A Love That Can't Be Contained

How to overflow with God's love through prayer, faith and action

Cally Magalhães

malcolm down

PUBLISHING

First published 2023 by Malcolm Down Publishing Ltd.
www.malcolmdown.co.uk

27 26 25 24 23   7 6 5 4 3 2 1

British Library Cataloguing in Publication Data
A catalogue record for this book is available from the British Library.

ISBN 978-1-915046-63-5

Cover design by Angela Selfe
Art direction by Sarah Grace

Printed in the UK

Dedication

For Connie, my dear friend and sister in Christ.
Thank you for your shining example and all that you have taught me.
So much of who I am and what I do is because of you.

His authority on earth allows us to dare to go to all the nations. His authority in heaven gives us our only hope of success. And His presence with us leaves us no other choice.[1]

1. John Stott in Randy Alcorn, *It's All About Jesus* (Eugene, OR: Harvest House Publishers, 2020). Original source unfound.

Endorsements

This is truly the most accessible and authentic resource for sharing the uncontainable love of God with non-religious people. Cally is a humble and inspiring guide throughout, drawing on her own stories of mistakes as well as marvels. This will be the first book I'll give from now on to anyone who wants to become a missionary in contexts near and far. It is a terrific manual for anyone who wants to share the message, mercy, and miracles that speak of the Father's limitless love.

Mark Stibbe, award-winning author of A Book in Time. *Award-winning fiction writer, ghost writer, and CEO of BookLab*

Cally's beautiful surrendered heart to Jesus shines so brightly in our troubled world. In her book, Cally shows us what a life wasted on Jesus looks like. What it means to be His hands and feet, carrying his love and compassion to the broken-hearted, the outcast, the poor and marginalised, those without hope. Through her acts of kindness and simple obedience to God's nudges, she sees him use her to transform those around her in the most amazing and miraculous ways. Cally invites you to discover how you can be God's messenger of love to those broken, lonely and lost around you. As you step out, you will never be the same again.

Cally inspires and challenges us to step out of our comfort zone and allow God to use us to bring his love and comfort to a hurting world. Cally's life is a beautiful example of radical love for Jesus. Like Mary of Bethany, she has broken her vase and poured her life out on Jesus, through loving the poor, the outcasts, the marginalised, and this fragrance of love has touched many hearts and changed many lives. As you read her stories, you too will learn the secret of this love that can't be contained.

Connie Calder, evangelist, former national executive team – YWAM England
and Andrew Taylor, former national elder – YWAM England

Cally Magalhães has often been asked when she's going to get a proper job. If trusting God completely with her life, flying out to the favelas of São Paulo and founding a ground-breaking, life-changing charity working with young men in the youth prisons isn't a proper job then I don't know what is. Her second book is written in the genre I'm calling missionary memoir, taking the reader from her very first experiences of mission and her growing reliance on God and it's totally gripping. Each chapter ends with a set of gently challenging questions. Beautifully written and totally unputdownable, I absolutely loved it and so will you.

Ruth Leigh, freelance writer, novelist and creative writing coach

An eye-opening, page-turning, potentially life-changing personal account of working with the poor and marginalised in short-term and long-term missions. Cally's story, and the helpful questions found at the end of the chapters, will encourage the reader to think about and respond to God's call on their own life. Moving, challenging and inspirational.

Sheila Jacobs, editor, award-winning writer, author of A Little Book of Rest

Contents

Foreword

WYSIWYG *(What You See Is What You Get)* comes to mind when I think of Cally Magalhães. She is an ordinary person, called by an extraordinary God to come alongside ordinary, overlooked people to do extraordinary things with divine assistance.

I first met Cally through my wife. They encountered each other when Frances worked for the UK Christian charity Stewardship. Subsequently, Frances has keenly and prayerfully followed Cally's unique ministry and has often regaled incredible stories of God at work in and through this faithful disciple of Christ. When I spoke with Cally myself and interviewed her at Methodist Central Hall Westminster, I realised what a humble and inspiring woman she is – living by faith and exercising total trust in her heavenly Father. What's more, reading her first book *Dancing With Thieves*, I was deeply impressed by her heart for justice and belief that restoration is possible and necessary. Clearly, her work in recent years with street kids and in youth prisons in Brazil is not only respected but bearing much fruit.

The founder of the Methodist movement, John Wesley, had a list of rules for Methodist evangelists. Rule 11 in the 1753 version reads: 'You have nothing to do but to save souls. Therefore, spend and be spent in this work. And go always not to those who need you, but to those who need you most.'

If Cally were a Methodist, I'm confident John Wesley would consider her an obedient and effective evangelist! Clearly, God uses Cally's gifts and skills as a teacher and courageous leader to bring compassion, healing, transformation and faith to many people. What's more, she is a great storyteller who testifies to the adventure of sharing in God's mission with a warmth, honesty and relatability that is infectious and challenging. I am sure you will find this compelling book easy to read. Its profound simplicity has undoubtedly impacted my soul.

I'd also recommend this book for small groups to read and ponder together. Each chapter ends with helpful and thought-provoking questions, and QR code links to videos which will aid reflection and stimulate discussion. I am confident that many will hear God calling them to engage in mission work because of *A Love That Can't Be Contained*.

Bless you, Cally. May God continue to protect you, provide for you, keep you and use you powerfully to make a difference!

Rev Tony Miles
Broadcaster, author and superintendent minister
Methodist Central Hall Westminster, London

A Note from the Author

Dear friend,

I am so glad you are reading this book. It's the second book I have written, and I still can't really believe I am writing these words. I never imagined I would even write one book, let alone a second.

The experience of writing this book, however, has been a very different experience from the first, as whilst working on *Dancing with Thieves*[2] I had so many doubts about my writing ability. I kept telling myself: You need to give up, you don't know how to write, no one will want to read it!

However, I am so happy with how it turned out and the reaction from people who have read it. I'm also so encouraged as recently the Portuguese version of the book won first place in the autobiography/biography category for the Areté Prize, the biggest Christian literature prize in Latin America. Even more amazing is that it was chosen from three years of entries as there were no prizes given since 2019 because of the COVID-19 pandemic. That alone encourages me to keep going, and I can honestly say I have enjoyed every minute of writing this book!

A Love That Can't Be Contained is for those who long for a deeper relationship with the Lord, and if you have a desire to find practical ways to share your faith on a day-to-day basis, or serve God in missions, then this book is for you.

I really hope my words will encourage and inspire you in your journey with God, and the mission He has for you here on this earth. That mission might be in your hometown or in

---

2. Cally Magalhães, *Dancing With Thieves* (Welwyn Garden City: Sarah Grace Publishing, 2020).

another nation or nations, but one thing is certain, God has a mission for your life.

If you are interested in going deeper, there are questions at the end of the chapters based on the theme of each one, so it can easily be used as a study book for you individually or with small groups of adults or young people. If you use it as a group, I suggest you aim to read a chapter before each meeting and then come together to discuss and pray together about what you have read. You may also wish to click on the QR code at the end of each chapter and watch a short video by me, based on the content.

You may have read my first book, *Dancing With Thieves*, and already know many details about my life and especially my work as a missionary in São Paulo, Brazil. I would love to encourage you to read it if you haven't already, but here is a quick recap on the last fifty-eight years of my life.

I was born in Harpenden, England in 1964. I trained as a dancer, and then worked as a professional actress and teacher. I lived in Kent for several years and it was there that I became a Christian after the break-up of my first marriage, before moving to Milton Keynes in 1991.

I began working at a large comprehensive school and while teaching there felt a real need to study the Bible. I so wanted to share Jesus with people, and felt I needed to understand the Bible better so that I knew how to explain my faith more clearly. I went to King's Bible College in Scotland for a year (now situated in Oxford) and then did the Discipleship Training School with YWAM[3] in Estonia. I also went on short-term mission trips to India and Bosnia. I sensed my life would be dedicated to long-term mission somewhere – I just didn't know where.

---

3. Youth With A Mission, https://ywam.org/ (accessed 10 January 2023),

In 1994 I read a magazine article about street kids in São Paulo and was deeply moved by their situation. God touched my heart powerfully and for weeks afterwards I felt very strongly that He was calling me to Brazil. I began to pray, and asked Him to confirm this call – which He did, several times.

At that time, I had set up a ministry in Milton Keynes called 'Signpost for Schools', working in primary schools with a team, presenting assemblies with Christian themes. I felt I couldn't leave until I had a successor and so trained up a young man, Daniel Crook, to carry on the work after I left, which he did for ten years, working in forty schools and talking monthly to about 10,000 children!

In 1998 I finally made my first visit to São Paulo and spent one month working in a *favela* (slum). On the last day I met George, a young Brazilian man who didn't speak English. As I didn't speak hardly any Portuguese, it was just 'Hi' and 'Bye', but he caught my eye, and I caught his!

I returned to England and felt certain God was indeed calling me to Brazil. I did a TESOL[4] course, packed my two suitcases and returned to Brazil in January 1999. Friends asked me if I was going for one year or maybe two years, and my heartfelt reply was, 'No, I'm going forever!'

I began working in a *favela*, teaching English and visiting the families. In my first week there were nine people murdered. However, I loved being there and felt no fear. I had no idea if I was visiting the main drug trafficker, criminals etc. – I just tried to show God's love to everyone I met.

I had been single for nine years and longed to be married again. I began to pray earnestly for a husband. In March of 1999, George went to the missionary hostel where I was living to meet a team making a film in the *favela*, and we met again.

---

4. Teaching English to Speakers of Other Languages.

We began to go out and fell in love, and four months and eleven days later we were married.

After our marriage in November 1999, we began working on the streets with the street kids and adults in the *favelas* and occasionally visiting the prisons. We witnessed God do miracles and saw many people become Christians and receive healing. In June 2001 our first son, Benjamin, was born and then Joseph two years later.

In 2004 one of our street boys who was very special to us was arrested and put in the youth prison. Staff from another organisation in São Paulo were helping him but when they lost their funding, asked if we could start visiting him. That was when our work in the youth prisons officially began and in 2006 we founded a non-governmental organisation called Associação Águia (The Eagle Project).

For six years we worked in various youth prison units, visiting the boys and working with their families, and taking them to rehabilitation centres where they began a new life without drugs or returning to crime. We found that many times, however, a rehab wasn't the right place for the boys straight after youth prison as they wanted their freedom. Many ran away a few days after their arrival and it became obvious that we needed a different strategy.

In 2012 I began to pray for a more effective way to help these boys and I felt God was leading us to start a new programme. As a result, we began a new project called 'Breaking the Chains' – using psychodrama workshops based on Restorative Justice with groups of boys in the youth prison to help prepare them for their release. (I did a post-graduate course for two years in psychodrama in São Paulo – it was the hardest thing I have even done – especially writing my thesis of 21,000 words in Portuguese!)

In 2013 we were nominated and accepted as part of the Inspired Individuals project sponsored by Tearfund, receiving financial support, coaching and the opportunity to network with others around the world working with youth at risk. This included meetings in Guatemala, South Africa, the UK, Colombia, Argentina and Costa Rica. We were even invited to meet Prince Harry to talk about our work during an event at the British Consulate, and met Archbishop Desmond Tutu in Cape Town, South Africa!

In 2014 my marriage with George began to fall apart, and sadly in 2017, we were divorced. It was a very difficult time, but God has been so faithful.

The project with psychodrama in the youth prison has now been running for ten years. The boys also receive individual counselling from our team, and we visit them and their family after their release, supporting in whatever way we can and helping them to find work or study at university. Psychodrama is an incredible tool and in 2022 the Brazilian Federation of Psychodrama awarded us first prize for our work in the youth prisons.

The project is growing – we are now leading groups weekly in four youth prisons and have a waiting list to start the project in other prison units. I have a great team and there are eleven of us – all Brazilians except me. We have also recently begun a pilot project working with prison directors and staff, caring for the carers, due to the extremely high rate of suicide among prison workers.

In 2022 I was invited to give a lecture at the University of São Paulo, considered the top university in Brazil, teaching law students with the theme 'Restorative practices behind bars'.

I am also very encouraged and excited that my first book, *Dancing with Thieves*, has been translated and published in Portuguese, hopefully also to be released in Spanish, and is soon to be made into a film by Dean Owen-Sims and Eternal Entertainment Ltd. God really does 'do immeasurably more than all we ask or imagine, according to his power that is at work within us' (Ephesians 3:20).

That was a quick recap. I hope it helps you understand some of the locations and people in my stories. I have changed the names of some of those mentioned to protect their identities.

Enjoy!

Introduction

'What a waste!' the young man yelled. He pointed at the slender young woman kneeling beside him, and all eyes turned in his direction. Contempt and ridicule were in his eyes and the expression on his face was twisted and cruel.

Now everyone in the room was staring at her. Some were seated on wooden benches, others reclined on large floor cushions. There was a hubbub of conversation and those in the doorway pressed in, curious to see what was happening.

'That perfume was worth a year's wages!' the same man yelled. 'It could have been sold at a high price and given to help the poor!' He lifted his chin with an arrogant air as if he knew all there was to know about money. Several of the men around him mumbled in agreement.

By this time the young woman on her knees was quickly undoing the plait in her long, thick hair. She fumbled as she tried to separate the strands and shook out her locks which tumbled gracefully over her shoulders.

'There's perfume everywhere,' she said to herself, now using her hair to wipe her master's feet, attempting in vain to mop up the perfume that was already beginning to drip onto the floor. 'I've made a big mess, and I don't care,' she thought, her heart beating fast as she continued to wipe his feet. Her face and neck were crimson, and she could feel 100 eyes boring into her back. 'I didn't think this through, I didn't think I would make this much mess, but I did what I wanted to. I poured out all my perfume, because I love him so much and that's what he deserves. I gave him my all. He's everything to me, and I don't care what they think.'

She stood up slowly, her hair now a tangled and sodden mess. She looked down and saw that perfume was dripping in lines down both the front and the back of her plain linen dress.

The air was thick with the intoxicating fragrance of the perfume, and out of the corner of her eye she could sense everyone in the room inhaling deeply as they relished the smell. Even her attackers. It was impossible not to be stirred by the exquisite aroma, so sweet and yet so pungent.

She caught her sister's eye. She was perched on the edge of her seat and staring at her with an expression of both surprise and admiration. They smiled at each other, and Mary knew instantly that her sister understood. Their brother too had a look of astonishment on his face, shaking his head with his mouth open wide. He winked at her as if to say, 'Well done, sis,' but she could tell he was thinking, 'Now look what you've done!' The mumbling ceased and silence hung in the air for a few seconds.

She lifted her head, pulled back her shoulders in defiance and waited. The man, the recipient of this extravagant act of sacrifice, looked at her carefully for a few seconds, and then his lips broke into a broad smile. His eyes smiled too and lit up His whole face.

She wondered what he was going to say.

'Leave her alone,' he turned to the crowd and announced. 'What she has done is so important. The poor will always be with you, but she has prepared me for My burial.'

'Burial?' she winced. 'I'm not sure the perfume will last that long. Why is He talking about His burial?'

At that moment she didn't want to think about His death. She just wanted to think about life. About living for Him.

About loving Him with all that she had. She felt His pleasure and it felt so good.

The snarling, contemptuous man lowered his head and skulked off into a corner of the room. She inhaled deeply, savouring every moment of that perfume, smiling at her master, so content she had 'wasted' it all on Him.

This Bible story, found in John 12:1-8, is very special to me. I was chosen to play the role of Mary, the woman who anointed Jesus, in 'The Mystery Plays at Canterbury Cathedral' in 1986. I was just embarking on my career as a professional actress and was excited to be given such an important role. I wasn't a Christian at the time, and I know I would play this role with so much more understanding now if I had the chance. I do remember, however, being full of admiration for this woman and her courageous act of sacrifice.

Years later I heard my dear friend Connie Taylor speak about Mary and her outpouring of love at my YWAM Discipleship Training School in Estonia. Connie is an evangelist, powerfully anointed by God, and I was so impacted by what she shared. She talked about 'wasting' our lives on Jesus and my life was never the same again.[5]

I decided that day to 'waste' my life on Jesus. To 'waste' my time, my money, my energy, my everything. Mary's attitude and act of love moves me deeply. She wasn't concerned for what others thought. She didn't think twice about pouring out all of the perfume. She could have chosen to pour out just a few drops, or maybe slightly more, but no, she chose to break the vase and 'waste' all that she had.

The breaking of the vase is also significant to me. There was no going back, no saving some perfume for herself, or another occasion. It was total and radical abandonment, total and

---

5. After hearing Connie's talk I went to my room and wrote a song (see Appendix One).

radical love. I don't know why she loved Jesus so much. Maybe it was because He raised her brother, Lazarus, from the dead? I don't have the answer but one thing I know – it is with that kind of love that I want to live my life for Jesus.

I have dedicated my life to serving God as a missionary, and on various occasions have faced criticism and ridicule. I have been asked, 'When are you going to get a proper job?' and my father's dying words to me were, 'Don't you think you're just scratching the surface?'

In reply to the first question about the *proper job* the answer is simple. My life as a missionary isn't a 'job', it's a privilege. I'm not seeking a career or material riches. My eyes are on Jesus, and my one desire is to follow Him.

And my answer to my father was, 'Yes, in many ways I am just scratching the surface, Dad, but if no one scratches the surface, nothing will ever change.'

My yearning for a worldwide prison system that is restorative instead of merely punitive is such a huge challenge. It certainly is so much bigger than me, but if I can make just a small difference, scratching the surface a little more each day, then I'm going to keep on trying until things change.

This book is about that radical love that Mary showed, a 'love that couldn't be contained'. A love that she decided to pour out in order to show how much she loved Jesus. I also want to pour out that love day after day to show my love for Him, and for those He places in my path.

This book is intended to challenge you, to call you higher and deeper into Him than you could ever imagine. It is intended to help you step out of your comfort zone, take that 'alabaster vase' in your hands and break it.

Are you willing to pour out the perfume of your life, breaking your vase of love without restraint, radically, wholeheartedly and unashamedly? Are you ready to give yourself to Jesus, allowing His fragrance in your life to powerfully permeate the lives of others? Are you willing to live for Him? Are you also prepared to risk stepping out for Him and trust that He will take care of you? Many of the stories here are about God's miraculous and incredible protection, provision and care. I pray that this book not only encourages you to step out and love others more, but also to have a deeper understanding of God's love for you.

This book is also about 'being', not just 'doing'. I encourage you to ask God: 'Lord, what can I *be* for You today?' Note, not 'What can I *do*?' but 'What can I *be*?'

'Jesus, let me *be* Your eyes today, to see the need around me. Show me those who so desperately need a touch from You.

'Let me *be* Your ears, to actively listen to those who long to be heard. Open my ears to purposely listen to Your voice, and act on what I hear.

'Father, let me *be* Your lips today, to speak with love, truth and grace and *be* a channel for Your peace. Lord, please give me the gift of prophecy[6] to speak Your word into people's lives. My desire is to sing Your praises and worship You with all my heart. Anoint me to use my words and my lips to encourage, to bless and to edify.

'Lord, let me *be* Your feet today. Allow me to go where You want to take me, at Your pace and not mine. Please, Lord, take my feet where You desire to walk and allow me to bring Your radiant beauty to those places.

'Lord, let me *be* Your arms today, to embrace and hold those who so need to receive Your love. Use me to wrap Your arms around the unloved, the hurting and the lonely. Teach me to make my embrace long and lingering so Your embrace may be felt through me.

---

6. Prophecy is a spiritual gift given by God to communicate to His people. See 1 Corinthians 12:7-11; 1 Corinthians 13:2; 1 Corinthians 14.

'Lord, may the beat of my heart *be* in time with Your heartbeat today. Fill me to overflowing so that I might love intentionally and unconditionally. I allow my heart to be broken with the things that break Your heart.

'I love You, Lord, with all my heart, my soul, my mind and my strength.'

Dear friend – I pray for you that as you pray in this way, and as you read this book, a 'love that can't be contained' will well up inside you and flow out of you and through you to the broken world around you.

Questions

1. What were your thoughts and impressions as you read the Introduction?

2. Think about something you did recently or in the past to show God's love to someone. What happened?

3. Have you faced criticism or ridicule for your faith? What was your reaction?

4. How do you listen to God's voice?

5. Note down and pray about one or two things in your life that you could change or need to change in order to 'waste' your life on Jesus.

6. Think about one way you intend to *be* Jesus to someone in the next few days.

Click on the QR code to watch the video about this chapter

Chapter One:

Be Open to God's Call

He said to them, 'Go into all the world
and preach the gospel to all creation.'
(Mark 16:15)

Do you have those moments or times in your life when God showed you something or did something that you will never forget? As I look back over the last thirty-two years of my life as a follower of Christ, I can pinpoint certain moments when I know with absolute certainty that He was speaking to me or leading me in a certain way.

In *Dancing With Thieves*, I describe a life-changing moment when I saw hundreds of homeless adults and children sleeping on the station platforms of Bombay.[7] That tragic scene opened my eyes to poverty and homelessness in a way that revolutionised my thinking and attitudes forever. However, that wasn't the only life-changing moment on that trip.

To be honest with you, India isn't a country I would have naturally chosen to visit. There are many other destinations I would much to prefer to visit, like Bali, Switzerland, Hawaii or Australia.

In the first place, I'm not a fan of very hot weather and secondly, kormas or tandooris are about my limit of spice.

---

7. Magalhães, *Dancing With Thieves*, pp. 37-38.

However, I really liked the idea of being part of a mission trip with the worship team from my church and so decided to sign up. It was 1992 and I was still a relatively new Christian so imagined I would just be there to carry the suitcases and be a general helper.

The first few seconds in Bombay were a huge shock. I shuffled along the aisle in the direction of the plane exit door, waiting patiently as the other passengers grabbed their hand luggage and belongings. It felt so good to stretch my legs after such a long flight.

As I stepped out of the plane onto the first rung of the steps, a tsunami of dry heat smacked me in my face and almost knocked me backwards. I gasped for breath and felt like I had just walked into a sauna. Then, as I took another deep breath, an overwhelming stench of fish hit me like a second tsunami. Bombay is a port, today known as Mumbai, and the smell of fish is staggeringly strong.

I struggled across the tarmac, pulling my hand luggage behind me and wiping away the river of perspiration forming on my brow. The heat was overpowering and felt like nothing I had ever experienced before.

'I'm not sure this trip is going to be easy,' I thought to myself. I then felt guilty. 'Yes, but I didn't sign up to have fun. Here I am, God, to serve You in India. I really do want to serve You, but I didn't think it would be this hot!'

The team members around me were struggling too, huffing and puffing as they tried to make their way to the baggage claim. I was impressed with all the different styles of luggage moving slowly along the revolving conveyor belt. There were conventional suitcases, huge floppy cloth bags full of swathes of different materials and half-collapsed cardboard boxes with their contents spilling out.

Eventually, we all retrieved our luggage and pushed our trolleys in the direction of the exit doors. There were hundreds of people jostling and pushing, almost everyone going in different directions. Women and girls were dressed in bright-coloured saris and *shalwar kameez*,[8] their black hair pulled back into plaits and ponytails. Others were dressed in tailored, fitted suits with expensive-looking handbags, with sleek, dark hair. Men were dressed in typically Indian outfits too and others in three-piece suits.

'How do they manage to work in this intense heat, dressed like that?' I thought to myself.

Arriving on the pavement outside the airport, we were greeted by Pastor Samuel, a young Indian man with a wide smile and very white teeth. My nostrils were still being accosted by the incredibly strong smell of fish now mixed with the fragrance of perfume, incense, spices and sweat.

'Welcome to India, my brothers and sisters, and welcome to Bombay,' Pastor Samuel announced. He flagged down some taxis and we all jumped in, unaware we were just about to begin our next adventure. If I thought the heat was bad, now I was in for a new challenge.

The traffic was chaos! Taxis, cars, rickshaws, motorbikes, combis, bicycles and pedestrians raced along the roads, each one fighting for their own space and position. Horns blared in a constant cacophony of sound, and I realised they were the replacement for indicators, as it was obvious no one was using them. Our taxi driver wove in and out of the traffic, deftly avoiding the other road users, including cows, chickens and stray dogs.

I had just begun to relax a little when without warning it began to rain. It was the monsoon season, and the late

---

8. The typical Indian matching tunic and trousers.

afternoon rain began to fall so hard it was like a waterfall crashing over the car. The heaviest rain I had ever seen began filling up the roads in a matter of seconds, the noise on the car roof so loud we could hardly make ourselves heard. In the next few moments something happened that I had never witnessed before, and never have since.

The taxi driver rolled down his window and then took a windscreen wiper out of the glove compartment. Holding it firmly in his hand he stretched his arm out of the window and began to wipe the windscreen. I realised to my dismay that his windscreen wipers were broken, and obviously this was the best alternative. He was a short man and could hardly reach the pedals, let alone stretch his arm out of the window. He was now using his other hand to both change gear and steer, at the same time as desperately trying to wipe the windscreen to see where he was going.

Thoughts of death began to run through my mind: 'Does this man realise I have parents who love me, friends who will miss me, a life to live ahead of me? I can't die in this taxi; I've only just arrived!'

I honestly wondered if I was going to get through this alive. The situation was crazy. We were now on a main road and travelling at high speed in torrential rain, with a taxi driver who was clearly oblivious of our fear and was doing too many activities with too few hands. Each time he changed gear, he had to take his hand off the steering wheel and with his other hand out of the window, the car swerved and lurched almost out of control. I threw my hands over my face and watched the scene in terror through the gaps in my fingers.

After what seemed like a few hours, but were only in fact a few minutes, we drew up in front of the hostel where we were to be staying. It was a hostel for backpackers and to give it a one-star rating would be extremely generous. Nevertheless, it was a roof over our heads and a bed for the night. Just to be on firm ground was a huge relief and I pulled my luggage out of the boot of the taxi with immense gratitude to be alive. By the time we reached the door of the hostel we were completely drenched; we had to leap across a deep pool of water from the taxi to the door.

The hostel was extremely dirty and falling apart. The bedroom looked like it hadn't been cleaned for a decade. I lay down in my bed that night, exhausted from the flight and the journey. Just as I was dropping off to sleep my friend Diana who was sharing a room with me declared in her wonderful Birmingham accent, 'Cally, I've been thinking.'

'Yes, Di,' I replied sleepily. 'What is it?'

'Well, maybe this is the punishment.'

'Punishment, Di?' I asked, curious as to what she meant.

'Yes, Cally, this is the punishment – I just don't remember the crime!'

We laughed loudly and soon fell asleep.

The next week was full of wonderful new experiences, challenges and perspiration! The Indian people were so welcoming and kind, and the church members treated us with overwhelming hospitality. I learned a lot about generosity and sacrifice that week and was confronted daily with the reality of my privileged middle-class upbringing and education.

As a new Christian I felt stretched and challenged in so many different ways. I realised how being on mission was like being planted in a greenhouse, growing much faster in my faith than I would back home. I loved the opportunity to sing with the worship team and experience the presence of God so powerfully with my new Indian brothers and sisters. Nothing, however, could have prepared me for what was to come.

At the end of the first week, we travelled eight hours by bus to the south of India and a little town nestling in the mountains.

It was breathtakingly beautiful and such a contrast to the hustle and bustle of Bombay. Much of the journey was along narrow winding roads with hairpin bends and steep mountain passes. I was horrified to see so many lorries and buses literally hanging over the edge of the road on many of the bends and prayed hard that we would make it without incident.

On our arrival, we were received like royalty and settled into our new accommodation, so much cleaner than the backpackers' hostel. The pastor's home was comfortable and homely and surrounded by beautiful plants and fragrant flowers. The small town nestled into the side of a mountain and the air was clean and pollution-free. It felt like a different world from the centre of Bombay.

The first day was spent getting to know the pastor and his wife and chatting and praying together as a team. The pastor was a quietly spoken but fervent man of God and the way he prayed filled me with faith and excitement. His wife was gentle and kind and kept asking if we were OK and bringing us cold water to quench our thirst.

That evening the leader of our team informed us that the next day we would be leading two assemblies at a large school in the town. The headteacher was a devout Christian man and was keen for us to share about Jesus with the students.

We would do two presentations – the first for the younger children, aged five to eleven years, and the second for the students aged between twelve to eighteen. He suggested that we sang some songs and then one of us could give a talk. We could also invite the older children to give their lives to Christ, as the headteacher had their parents' consent.

He felt that the younger children maybe wouldn't understand the significance of what they were doing and asked us to only invite the older students to make a commitment. Everyone agreed and I could tell the team was excited about this new challenge.

There was a lull in the conversation and our team leader looked across the room at me and said with a smile on his face, 'Cally, I would like you to speak at the two assemblies, please.'

'Me?' I exclaimed. 'I don't know what to say! Can't someone else do it?'

'No, I think this one is with you, Cally,' he replied calmly, and I realised he wasn't going to change his mind.

Then began hours of prayer, fretting and fervent preparation. This was all new to me and I was totally out of my comfort zone. I hardly slept that night, going over and over in my brain the words I would say. The next day I woke up exhausted but also excited to step out into this new experience and see what God would do. The privilege of possibly helping these children to know Jesus as their Saviour was all-consuming, and I felt a deep sense of responsibility.

We left for the school and the van took us through winding roads lined with flaming red, pink and orange bougainvillea. On arrival we were welcomed by the headteacher, a tall, gentle Indian man, obviously passionate about his school and students.

The first assembly was a success. The children loved the songs and the presentation, joining in shyly at first and then more enthusiastically. We taught them the hand and arm movements to go along with the words and they seemed to love every moment. We were mobbed by the whole group at the end of the assembly until the headteacher shooed them along to their classrooms.

Then it was time for the older children. They filled the school hall, quietly filing into their seats, a gentle hubbub of whispers and giggles. As soon as the presentation began, they joined in with enthusiasm, obviously enjoying the experience and singing the songs with gusto.

Now it was my moment and I spoke the message that I felt God had prompted me to share. I wanted to encourage them to know God as their Father and to understand that He loved each one of them so much.

'I want to tell you a story,' I said. 'Once there was a man who a famous tightrope walker. He was very brave and skilled and did some incredible feats, walking his tightrope across mountain ravines and other very high places.'

The children had fallen silent and were listening intently to every word.

'One day he went to New York and tied his rope between two skyscrapers,' I continued. 'A skyscraper is the name given to buildings that are so high it looks as though they are scraping the sky.' The children looked at each other in amazement and gasped. I realised how so many of these children lived a very isolated life out in this mountainous region without access to the outside world. Their big brown eyes stared at me, hanging on my every word.

'Then the man took a long deep breath, and started to walk across the rope,' I went on. 'A huge crowd began to form on the street below as passers-by stood motionless with their mouths wide open, gazing at the spectacle above.'

I stood frozen on the stage with my head tilted back and my mouth wide open as if I was one of the passers-by. The students roared with laughter. I waited for their laughter to subside and continued, my voice now louder and more dramatic than before.

'It was a windy day, and the rope began to swing, and the man began to wobble. The crowd fell silent, not knowing if he would fall at any moment. Slowly and carefully, he continued to walk across the rope and a few moments later,' I paused for effect, 'he reached the other side, jumping triumphantly onto the ledge beside him. The crowd shouted and applauded, and everyone cheered with delight.'

The children all clapped too, totally immersed in the story. The applause died down and I lowered my voice almost to a whisper. 'Suddenly they heard him call down to the crowd and fell silent as they tried to hear what he was saying. "One of you come up here now," he shouted, "and I will walk across the rope with you sitting on my shoulders!"

'"What?" the onlookers said to each other.

'"I'm not going to do that!" said one.

'"Nor me," another agreed. "That is way too dangerous."

'Suddenly from out of the crowd a young boy pushed his way through to the side of the building and began to climb the ladder to reach the man.

'"What is he doing?" a woman cried.

'"He must be mad!" another exclaimed.

'Still the boy kept climbing until he reached the man and stepped carefully onto the rope beside him. The man whispered some instructions in his ear and then swung the boy up onto his shoulders. Very slowly they started to walk across the tightrope.

'The crowd was completely silent as each person looked up at the man and the boy, holding their breath in anticipation. Even the buses and cars in the street had stopped, and the drivers were staring into the sky alongside the pedestrians.'

I looked at the sea of faces before me and every child was transfixed, their eyes staring in astonishment.

'The wind continued to blow and several times the man had to pause to keep his balance. Now he wasn't only risking his own life but also the life of this young child. After what seemed like several minutes but was in fact just a matter of seconds, they reached the other side and the crowd exploded in a round of applause.'

The children also roared and cheered, and I laughed to myself at their fascination with this story. I was enjoying myself and enjoying their reaction.

'A few moments later, the boy was back on firm ground and the crowd gathered around him, patting him on the back and cheering loudly. The boy was grinning, obviously enjoying his newfound fame.

'An elderly lady pushed her way through the crowd until she stood before him and asked, "Young man, how did you do that? That was incredible. Tell me. How did you trust that man?"

'The young boy smiled. "It was easy, ma'am," the boy replied confidently.

'He paused. The crowd was silent, waiting for his reply.

'"He's my dad!" he cried.

There was a moment of silence in the assembly hall and then all the children gasped and clapped, loving the story and the surprise ending.

'So,' I explained, 'that little boy was able to trust that man because he was his father. And we are here to tell you today that God is our Father too and He loves us so much. He made each one of us and He longs for us to know Him as our dad. He sent His Son Jesus to die for us and to be our best friend.

'You can know God too and can ask Jesus to be your best friend today. To do that we need to ask God to forgive us, which means saying sorry for the things we've done wrong, and put our trust in Him.'

The children all looked at me, their big brown eyes shining, listening carefully to my every word. I took a deep breath. I so wanted them to put their trust in God and ask Jesus to be their Saviour.

'If you would like to pray and ask Jesus to be your best friend and Saviour, please come forward and we will pray with you.'

The team picked up their instruments and began to strum and play quietly. No one moved.

I waited.

My heart began to beat loudly, and I could feel the perspiration running down my back.

'Lord, please open their eyes to see You and to want to know You,' I prayed.

Again, I asked, 'If you would like us to pray with you, please come forward. I know it's a brave step to come to the front, but today you can put your life in God's hands and trust in Him.'

Once more no one moved. I waited again.

There was a long pause.

Suddenly, two of the younger boys who were seated by the wall and furthest away from the aisle began to shuffle with some difficulty past their classmates who were seated in the same row. Arriving in the aisle, they then walked to the front of the hall. They raised their hands and as they came, many other students came with them until there was a large group of children standing before me.

My knees began to wobble, and I felt a wave of emotions rising up inside me. Joy and exhilaration, excitement and thankfulness. This was one of the most amazing moments of my whole life. Witnessing so many children wanting to give their lives to Jesus was just the best thing possible.

'This is what I want to do for the rest of my life,' I whispered to God.

I led the children in a simple prayer, asking forgiveness from God and putting their lives in His hands. The children thanked us enthusiastically and the headteacher hurried them along to their classrooms, obviously happy with how the morning had gone.

The assembly was over, and I crumpled into a chair, overwhelmed by the whole experience. I felt an incredible sense of awe and a gratefulness for the power and kindness of God to touch these young children's hearts. I prayed they would indeed follow Him the rest of their lives.

That day changed me forever. That night as I lay down to sleep, I thanked God for the privilege of being in India, and for being able to serve Him, even though I was such a new Christian. I fell asleep wondering what other adventures the next days would bring.

Questions

1. Can you allow God to break your heart with the things that break His heart? What do you believe might happen if you do?

2. Would you be willing to serve God on a short-term mission trip? Where could you go and what would you like to do?

3. Are you open to God's call for long-term missions? Do you feel He has called you to a ministry, a certain nation or people group?

4. Modern missionaries often serve God in other nations by using their profession as a way of entering a country closed to the gospel. Why not pray about whether this is something God is leading you into?

5. Often Christians who feel called to full-time ministry (as in, leaving regular employment to preach the gospel in some sense) don't respond to the call for various reasons. Reflect on this.

6. You may not feel called to serve abroad. How can you be more involved in outreach/mission where you live?

Click on the QR code to watch the video about this chapter

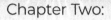

Chapter Two:

Be Ready for Anything

You have a God who hears you, the power of love
behind you, the Holy Spirit within you, and all of
heaven ahead of you. If you have the Shepherd, you
have grace for every sin, direction for every turn,
a candle for every corner and an anchor for every
storm. You have everything you need.[9]

We travelled back to Bombay a few days later, my mind still
reeling with images of the children at the school, their hands
raised, huge smiles on their faces as they gave their lives to
Jesus. I wondered what else God had in store for me in that place.

The day after we arrived back, I received an exciting
invitation. The church where we were staying had an outreach
team that taught school lessons to the street children, and
they were happy for me to accompany them the following day.
At that time, of course, I had no idea that years later I would
sense a very strong call from God and leave England to work
with the street children in São Paulo, Brazil.

I am a trained teacher, but I knew this was going to be a very
different experience from anything I had ever done before. The
only instruction I received was to stay close to the team, which
was comprised of two young Indian men and two middle-aged

---

9. Max Lucado, *Traveling Light: Premier Library Edition* (Nashville, TN: Thomas Nelson Inc, 2007).

Indian ladies. I was so excited I could hardly sleep that night, my mind buzzing with ideas of how I could help the children.

The next day I chose the lightest, coolest clothes I could find in my suitcase and met the team at the church. We set off to the station in two rickshaws and then travelled by train into the centre of the city. The train journeys in Bombay were always a fascinating experience but also a huge challenge. Maybe you have seen films or pictures of train carriages full to overflowing in India, but the reality is like nothing you can imagine.

The first challenge is the heat as you travel pressed up against people's bodies or more accurately, with your face in their armpits as you cling onto the overhead rail. I stood with the team, swaying with the movement of the train, perspiration dripping from my forehead to my toes.

The carriage was packed full of people, women carrying huge cloth bundles, babies staring wide-eyed and men conversing loudly. Every time we stopped at a station, about fifty more people boarded the train and we were squashed even tighter against our fellow passengers. Even when it seemed like the carriage was at bursting point, still more people squeezed themselves into the overcrowded space.

After about fifteen minutes my head began to feel incredibly light and for the first time in my life I wondered if I was going to faint. I licked the perspiration that was dripping into the corner of my mouth, hoping the salt would somehow make me feel better. It felt like I was in the hottest sauna possible but with no air. I was slightly separated from the other teachers and was so squashed I couldn't move in any direction. I began to call out weakly, 'Help! Help!'

A very large lady dressed in a bright orange sari immediately recognised my plight and began to push aside the bundles of cloth on the floor and elbow the people around me to make a small space.

'Make room, make room!' she cried, and people began edging away from me. The ladies from the team noticed the commotion and somehow manged to reach my side. They began fanning my face and pouring water on my neck. The large lady kindly gave up her seat on the wooden bench beside me and I sat down, very grateful for the assistance. She and my team members manoeuvred themselves into a position where they were able to create space in front of me, so I had some air to breathe. I was a little embarrassed at all the attention I was receiving but thanked them all profusely for the help.

Just the act of sitting down and finding some space to breathe made me feel a little better, and a few minutes later we arrived at our destination. The children were all waiting for us on the platform and waved madly at us through the train windows. We pushed our way through the passengers to jump off the train and were greeted by about twenty children, dressed in rags and squealing with delight.

'Come on everybody, follow us,' one of the female teachers cried, and hurried them along the platform. I rushed along with them, forgetting my near fainting fit, caught up with the excitement and enthusiasm of the children. I wondered what the rush was for and only discovered later that the school lessons for the street children were not a welcome activity by the railway authorities.

A few moments later we arrived at a large flight of stone steps and the children raced down them, arranging themselves neatly in organised rows. Their faces were bright and expectant and each one said 'Thank you, ma'am' as they received their notebook and pencil from the teachers.

A memory suddenly flashed into my mind. I remembered my students in England, and the challenge it was to inspire them to study. So many were disinterested and unwilling to learn, and several wouldn't even keep quiet and listen.

I recalled their brightly decorated classrooms with matching desks, adorned with fluorescent fluffy pencil cases overflowing with coloured pencils and pens.

I stared at the children before me, obviously so grateful for just one hour of school each day, like statues in the intense heat of Bombay. Their mouths were wide open, their teeth missing or rotten, hanging on every word the teacher was saying.

I sat down next to one of the boys, who shuffled along the step to make space for me.

'Sit here with me, Aunty,' he whispered. 'Then you can help me if I don't understand.'

'No problem, that's what I'm here for,' I whispered back.

He looked up at me, his big brown eyes shining brightly, his face and neck pitted with sores and insect bites. He was dressed in a pair of old ragged cotton shorts and a shirt that was so torn it was hanging in shreds. He must have been only about eight years old, and I wondered why he was living on a street instead of at home.

We sat listening to the teacher together.

'One times two is two,' the teacher chanted,

'One times two is two,' the children repeated.

'Two times two is four,' the teacher continued.

'Two times two is four,' the children repeated even more enthusiastically.

'I can do the twos,' my new friend whispered.

'Me *two*!' I whispered back and we both giggled at the play on words.

It all seemed very organised and under control and I sat back against the step, enjoying the experience, even though my heart was breaking for these children. I had great admiration for the team members, who were completely engrossed in the activities, and it was obvious they loved helping the children in this way.

I certainly wasn't expecting what happened next.

The normal hubbub of the station was broken by the sound of men's voices, shouting and grunting, and I looked round in the direction of the noise to see what was happening.

From around the corner at the top of the steps came several police officers, brandishing large wooden batons and bellowing at the tops of their voices. I had no idea what they were saying but they were obviously very angry.

We all jumped up and the children began screaming and shouting, their notebooks and pencils scattering down the steps. Some of the children were able to run away but others were already being beaten on their backs and arms by the policemen as they stumbled down the stairway.

'Don't worry, Aunty, I'll look after you,' my young friend announced confidently. 'Quickly, come with me. Don't be scared, I'll protect you.' He grabbed me by the hand and pulled me down the steps. My heart was beating fast as I scuttled alongside him, looking over my shoulder to see if the policemen were following us. They were not far behind, and I could see their faces twisted with hatred. I was shocked to be a witness of such violence towards these young children.

I remembered the instructions to stay close to the team and ran as fast as my legs would take me. My young friend had crooked his arm in mine and was almost propelling me along the platform. Within seconds we were outside on the pavement and reunited with the team and the other children.

I paused to catch my breath.

'Are you all right, Aunty?' my young friend asked, patting me gently on my arm.

'Yes, I'm fine,' I replied. 'What about you?'

'Yes, Aunty, I am fine, thank you very much,' he replied calmly, wobbling his head which made me wonder if he really was fine or not. 'This is normal for me,' he reassured me. 'I want to be a doctor, but it is so hard to study living on the streets.'

My attention was turned to the team members who were trying to negotiate with the policemen, but it was very clear they had no intention of allowing us to continue the lesson. They kept shouting the same words repeatedly, and it was obvious that school was finished for that day.

Some of the younger children were whimpering and others were rubbing their sore backs and shoulderss. The teachers were trying to bring a semblance of calm to the tense situation and some of the older children were comforting the little ones.

'Do the policemen always stop the lessons?' I asked one of the male team members.

'They're not policemen, they're the station guards,' he explained, 'and they hate the children because they steal and pickpocket. They do everything they can to keep them away from the station to avoid contact with the passengers. Of course, they can't stop them all the time, but they certainly don't like them to do school lessons here. Almost every time we come this happens,' he concluded sadly.

By this time the guards had gone back into the station, and the team were handing out snacks and drinks. Most of the children were seated on the pavement with their backs against the wall of the station and tucking into their snack with enthusiasm. It was now late in the afternoon and a very welcome breeze wafted across my hot neck and face.

'Thank you for looking after me,' I said to my new young friend, who was still holding my hand very firmly. I could feel his skin bumpy and rough against mine and squeezed his hand to show my appreciation.

'You're very welcome,' he said, squeezing my hand even tighter and putting his arm around my shoulder. We ate our snack together and he snuggled up against my side. All my ideas of what I was hoping to teach these children disappeared as I realised they were the ones who were teaching me.

A few minutes later we said our goodbyes and went back into the station. By this time, it was early evening and rush hour had already begun. Our train pulled in with a loud blow of a whistle, and we were carried along the platform like a tsunami tidal wave that delivered us through the doors and into the carriage. This time I seemed to be oblivious of the crush and the smell and the noise. All I could think of was twenty bright young children desperate to learn and being beaten for being 'at school'. I certainly had a lot to share with my disinterested students in the UK on my return!

A few days later another challenge was in store for me and for the whole team. We were invited to speak and lead worship one evening, at a church situated on the outskirts of the city. We all piled into rickshaws and set off on our journey. It was early evening and still very hot and humid. We laughed and chatted as we crossed the city, the rickshaws jiggling and rocking us from side to side.

Suddenly, without warning, the atmosphere changed, and the sky was filled with dark storm clouds. Seconds later the heavens opened, and the monsoon rain began to fall. The sides of the rickshaws were completely open to the elements, and we were lashed on both sides by the torrential rain.

The rickshaw drivers continued to battle through the streets but within a few minutes they had no choice but to give up. The roads were already deep with water, and they could continue no longer. A queue of rickshaws, cars and motorbikes had piled up in front of us and reluctantly we descended onto the street, stepping into the already deep water. Hastily I paid the driver for our journey, and we stood on the side of the road wondering what to do.

One of the leaders from the church who was escorting us encouraged us not to give up.

'Come on everybody, let's walk. The church isn't far from here,' he said. Two by two we paddled along, avoiding the street-sellers, and other pedestrians. Dogs and cows were also part of the procession, and I hoped we wouldn't get trodden on or bitten by an angry wet dog.

We hadn't thought to take umbrellas with us so within seconds we were drenched from head to foot. My sandals were making a strange squelching noise with each step that I took, and my clothes were sticking to my body.

I began chatting with one of the women on the team, a mum from the UK who was walking alongside her twelve-year-old daughter, Rebecca. Normally children that young weren't allowed on the team to India, but as her mum was there, she was allowed to take part.

Rebecca was small and slender, with long dark hair pulled back into a plait. I was impressed by her maturity and determination to keep up with the team during all the different activities of the trip. It was now almost over, and she certainly had had the experience of a lifetime.

Chatting and laughing at our latest challenge, we walked along the street, at times wading through knee-deep water. Suddenly, however, something terrible happened.

Without warning Rebecca disappeared. She had been walking by my side and then suddenly she wasn't there. I looked down and just saw a street full of rainwater. Where was Rebecca?

Had she been kidnapped? Did she get left behind? Was she lost? Where was she?

I didn't know what to do and began to panic, looking all around me and shouting her name.

Two seconds later her head bobbed up beside me in the water and we all shouted as a group of us grabbed her arms and clothes and hauled her to safety. We pulled her onto firm ground and gathered around her. A crowd of onlookers stopped to see, and people were shouting and gesticulating wildly.

Rebecca's mum was in a state of shock but miraculously Rebecca was fine. She had fallen down a drain hole which was completely out of sight due to the depth of the rain that had fallen so quickly. I learned later that people are employed specifically to pull out dead bodies from the drains there during the rainy season, as people fall into them with startling regularity.

Rebecca fortunately hadn't swallowed any of the water, which was a relief as it was obviously extremely dirty, and after a few minutes she was fine and able to keep walking to the church building. Now, the whole team were walking more slowly and stepping very carefully, so as not to fall down any drains. I was feeling quite shaky, but very relieved that Rebecca was alive and unharmed.

A few minutes later we arrived at the church, and were grateful to be able to shelter from the rain at last. Several church members had already begun to arrive. I was so impressed that they had all somehow managed to travel to the church in the monsoon rain without getting soaking wet like us.

The women looked so beautiful in their brightly coloured saris and trouser suits, their black hair sleek and shiny, and absolutely bone dry. I wondered what their secret was, but then saw a vast range of umbrellas in the doorway and made a mental note to remember to take my umbrella next time.

The pastor greeted us warmly, as did the church members, and the meeting was amazing that night. Several people gave their lives to Christ, and we worshipped God with such gratitude and love. We seemed to be oblivious of our soaking wet clothes and hair, just so extremely grateful that Rebecca was alive and well. She was feeling a little shaken up, and very wet, but otherwise fine after this incredible experience.

'That will be a story to tell your children and grandchildren,' I told her afterwards. 'It's not every day you fall down a drain in India and come out alive!'

This mission trip changed my life. I want to encourage you – go on mission trips, short term, long-term, in your home country, or in other nations. Don't make it complicated, just go! Your love for Jesus will grow, your faith will be stretched, and you will never be the same again.

Questions

1. Do you know any missionaries? How could you encourage them? By praying? By giving financially? By visiting them? By contacting them regularly? Pray about how you could be more involved and supportive.

2. Does your fear of danger or accident prevent you from stepping out and serving God in short-term or long-term missions? How can we overcome this fear?

3. What can we do to fight for justice in the world?

4. How about signing up for a short-term mission trip? You could do this through your church or through mission organisations.

5. Going on mission isn't easy. There are many challenges such as different foods, temperatures, getting along with team members, etc. What do you think would be most challenging for you in another nation, and how might you overcome this?

6. Can families be involved in missions? How? What are the challenges? What are the blessings?

Click on the QR code to watch the video about this chapter

Chapter Three:

Be Prepared to Be Blessed

You can never learn that Christ is all you need,
until Christ is all you have.[10]

I have been involved in missions for more than thirty years. I used to think that God was calling me to do missions in order to bless people. I have learned, however, that so often I am the one who receives the blessing.

In 1998 I had the opportunity to take part in a missions' trip to Bosnia. My church in Milton Keynes had a link with a church there and a trip was arranged to the formerly picturesque tourist town of Mostar.

The war, which started in 1992, had ended but the aftermath was enormous, and it was a very sad and moving experience. The war involved three people groups, the Bosnians, Serbs and Croats, and horrific ethnic cleansing occurred among them. When the war ended, they had to learn to live together again in peace. Not easy.

The church in Mostar and its adjacent Bible college had suffered considerable damage during the fighting. The pastor invited our church to take a team of builders to work on rebuilding the ruins, and I was keen to go along. I signed up to lead the street drama team and began to plan sketches and

10. Robert Ellsberg, *Blessed Among Us* (Collegeville, MN: Liturgical Press, 2016).

evangelistic presentations. A couple of weeks later, however, I received a message to say there wouldn't be a drama team after all. It was so soon after the end of the war and the country was in such chaos that it was considered too dangerous to witness openly on the streets. My building skills were minimal, so I agreed to head up the catering team. Having only ever cooked for a maximum of four people, I knew that cooking for twenty-four team members every day was going to stretch me to my limit. There was going to be a makeshift kitchen on the building site, and I knew that would be a challenge in itself. However, what most concerned me was how I was going to buy the food that we needed to cook.

'How am I going to go shopping and buy food if I can't speak the language?' I pondered. 'Lord, please help me learn at least some useful words before I go.'

A few days after praying this prayer I was talking to a local headteacher in Milton Keynes and mentioned the trip and my need to learn some of the Bosnian language.

'Well, I think I know someone who could help you,' he answered enthusiastically. 'We have a new student at the school and he and his mum, Anika, are from Montenegro.[11] I'll ask her if she can help. She could probably do with some extra cash, and you will at least have a few phrases under your belt before you leave.'

The following week I began my language lessons with my new-found Montenegrin friend. She was shy and softly spoken and able to speak very little English. I wondered what she had gone through that caused her to move to England and leave behind her life in Montenegro.

---

11. Montenegro is located on the Adriatic Sea, in the west-central Balkans, and has borders with Croatia, Serbia, Bosnia and Herzegovina, Kosovo and Albania.

'How can I help you?' she asked with a strong Montenegrin accent.

I imagined that I would need to say things like, 'Hello, please may I have a kilo of tomatoes, two kilos of potatoes,' etc., so I explained to her the words I needed to learn.

She helped me make a long list of the vocabulary and I practised the pronunciation repeatedly. It was no use knowing the words if no one was going to understand me. The Bosnian language sounds nothing like English, but after a couple of lessons I felt confident that I would be able to communicate.

The day after arriving in Mostar I made my first visit to the local market. There were stalls filled with different fruits and vegetables, some of which I recognised and some of which I had never seen before. The atmosphere was a little tense and people's expressions were filled with sadness and anxiety. After living for so many years in a state of tension, never knowing when they would be attacked or killed, it was going to take a while for this country to return to some semblance of normality.

The market traders shouted, encouraging the passers-by to pause, and I detected that the banter was over whose price was more appealing. Old women dressed in headscarves and long linen skirts held little cloth purses in their hands, trying to find just a few coins to pay for their purchases.

Complete with my list of vocabulary in my hand, I was able to communicate quite easily, and was grateful for the patience of the market traders. Some tried out their pidgin English on me and we laughed as we found ways to communicate some way or another, either with my list or with animated gestures. I was very satisfied that I was able to buy what I needed and very thankful for having met my language teacher ahead of time. 'Things could have been very complicated if I hadn't met Anika,' I thought to myself. 'I can't imagine having to mime all these fruits and vegetables. I think I may have caused a scene and drawn way too much attention to myself.'

I had an overwhelming sense of the graciousness of God who gave me this opportunity to prepare myself. In those days you didn't bump into people from the Balkans very regularly in the UK. God set me up, that was for certain.

The next month was an incredible experience as we got to know the local people and listened to their tragic stories. We heard about the war which was so unbelievably cruel as the ethnic groups of Bosnians, Serbs and Croats, formerly interwoven and living in peace, began to kill, rape and torture each other.

One of my most precious memories was of an elderly Muslim man called Amar. He was living in the bombed-out Bible college when we arrived, and the pastor had asked him to be responsible for the team and our work. He was a bit grumpy and didn't seem very happy that we would be there for the following few weeks. He was a tall, thin man, with a weather-beaten face, and short grey hair. He worked very hard on the building site and hardly stopped for food or drink.

The pastor told us his story. Before the war he was in a high position of authority in the Bosnian army and owned several houses with swimming pools, cars and lived a life of luxury. He was a Bosnian Muslim and when the war began, he was imprisoned by the Serbs and lost almost everything. His wife was evicted from their home and the Serbs took over their houses, cars and belongings.

Amar suffered so much in prison as he didn't know how his wife was coping, and the conditions and torture there were terrible. One night, however, something happened that changed his life. Jesus appeared to him in a dream and told him of his need for salvation – that he needed to believe in Him as his Lord and Saviour. Amar woke up and did just that – he became a Christian in the middle of the night in his prison cell! After that, Amar began to pray and ask Jesus to help him and specifically asked that God would bring about his release. A few months later, Amar was told he was to be set free. He was ecstatic but also extremely worried. He had heard a story that concerned him greatly, to the point of dreading his release.

Rumour had it that every time prisoners were liberated, three were chosen and sent out of the prison and down a long track. The guards who released them would stand outside the prison with their guns pointing at the newly released prisoners. Before the bend at the end of the road, one prisoner was always shot dead by one of the guards. Amar knew this and couldn't face the possibility of being the one who was murdered. He also couldn't imagine seeing either of his companions shot dead by his side.

He prayed and asked God for a miracle. A few hours later, his cell door was thrust open, and he and two fellow prisoners were dragged out. Their eyes stung as they were thrust into the sunlight and shoved through the half-open gate.

The guards glowered as Amar and the other two men half-walked, half-ran down the long, muddy track. The guards' guns were at shoulder-height pointing in their direction, and Amar sensed that their eyes were fixed on each one of them as they moved. Amar and his two companions linked their arms around each other's waists, united in fear, waiting for their fate.

Amar felt like his heart was beating in his throat, the sweat dripping down his face and neck. Each step he took led him closer to the bend and he felt as though his legs would give way beneath him. If he fell, surely he would be the one who was shot.

Suddenly, he could control himself no longer and shouted at the top of his voice, 'Jesus!'

The two others broke free, and began to run, certain that now they would all be shot. They approached the bend as Amar stumbled along behind them, frail and weak from so many months in prison. He could hardly walk, let alone run. Moments later they reached the bend in the road. They held their breath, waiting to hear the gunshot or the sound of the guards running after them. Silence hung in the air beneath the overhanging trees. The two men grabbed Amar by his armpits and practically propelled him along between them, laughing and crying at the same time.

'We're free,' Amar cried. 'Jesus saved us from death!' and they continued without stopping until they reached the next town.

The pastor told us this story and we wept with joy, for Amar's salvation and for the mercy of God in his life. As the days went by, he began to enjoy our company more and more, appreciating the gifts of chocolate and sweets that we had brought from England. I loved to see him smile, and we tried all different ways of making him laugh. I learned some more Bosnian words and phrases, and every day chatted with him for at least a few minutes.

We learned that he had lost almost everything and didn't even have his own cutlery. He lived in a small room on the site of the bombed-out Bible school with just a rickety old bed and a small wardrobe. This was a very different lifestyle from that to which he was accustomed.

The day before we left for the UK, I bought him a knife, fork and spoon and a couple of other small gifts and took them to him in his room. The door was open and when he saw me, he beckoned for me to go in. He was sitting reading his Bible and he greeted me with a friendly grin that made me feel like I wasn't interrupting.

I sat down beside him and placed the presents on his lap. When he opened the packet of cutlery, his eyes filled with tears, and he stood up quickly from where he had been sitting on his bed. He took me by the hand into a small storeroom next to his bedroom.

Opening an old, battered cardboard box he took out a plate, a teacup and a little pot, all in the same beautifully designed, typically Bosnian pottery. He placed them in my hands, and I said, 'Oh, they're lovely, Amar, lovely.'

'For you, for you,' he said, looking gently into my eyes and closing my fingers around the items of pottery.

'No, Amar, no, no,' I cried, shaking my head, trying to refuse the gifts. These were his few precious belongings, the only possessions he had, and he was giving them to me?

'Yes, yes,' he replied insistently, and then said something in Bosnian that he often said to me. He had a big smile on his face and said very clearly and slowly, '*Velike prijateljica*' – which means 'great friend'.

I looked down at the gifts and felt overwhelmed with gratitude for this precious man and all that he had taught me. I burst into tears, remembering weeks of weeping with heartbroken people, bombed-out homes and shops and schools, and three people groups terrified that the war wasn't truly over.

We both cried together as we said our goodbyes, and I have never forgotten those precious moments. Those pots have accompanied me in every house move ever since and now they have pride of place on the shelves of my apartment here in São Paulo.

The month I spent in Bosnia touched me more deeply than I could ever have imagined. I was so impressed at the power of God and the unity of the church in that place. Bosnians, Serbs and Croats regularly attended the worship meetings, praising and worshipping God together. Only in the church was that possible.

Amar taught me so much about forgiveness and faith, about overcoming and perseverance. He was such an example to me of someone who had owned so much but had learned to be content with almost nothing. I was so encouraged by his testimony and of the way his life was radically changed through his miraculous encounter with Jesus and His love. I returned to the UK with more faith than ever before, and wanting to pour out that love wherever God led me. I also reflected on how I had thought I was going to Bosnia to bless the people, but in fact the one who received the most blessings, was me!

Questions

1. Do you think short-term missions are more for us to grow as Christians than for the people we are serving? Why/why not?

2. Think about/share a time when you were the recipient of someone showing God's love to you.

3. Has God spoken to you through dreams?

4. There are many ways of showing God's love to someone. Which way/ways do you find the most comfortable?

5. How did you become a Christian? Write down your testimony or share it with someone.

6. 'It is more blessed to give than to receive' (Acts 20:35). Reflect on those words of Jesus.

Click on the QR code to watch the video about this chapter

Chapter Four:

Be Ready to Get it Wrong

For the Spirit God gave us does not make us timid,
but gives us power, love and self-discipline.

(2 Timothy 1:7)

I often get things wrong and end up feeling embarrassed. I have a series of funny stories about my blunders. However, it hasn't stopped me stepping out and making mistakes as I know, thankfully, that God uses my weaknesses and failures just as much as my abilities and gifts. He loves it when we take risks for Him.

Before I moved to São Paulo I lived in Milton Keynes, a town strategically positioned in the centre of the UK. I remember the advertisements on the TV for this town when it was being built. I was quite young and was fascinated by the images of happy people, clowns, hot-air balloons flying through the cloudless sky and the calm walkways and canals. It is indeed a very interesting town. It was very carefully planned to avoid traffic jams and has hundreds of roundabouts as part of a horizontal and vertical road system that keeps the traffic flowing.

My sons are used to sitting in traffic jams for hours here in São Paulo, so it was always a treat to visit Milton Keynes when they were younger and be able to travel quickly back and forth across the city. I recall one day sailing along the roads during rush hour and a voice from the back seat saying, 'Mum, is this Utopia?'

The grid system of roads also lends itself to a housing system of estates, and during the nine years that I lived in Milton Keynes I was a resident on one of them. The church I attended held its meetings at the local middle school and many of the church members lived on the estate. We were always keen to be a blessing to our neighbours and the residents of the estate and organised many different evangelistic events and activities.

On Mother's Day we divided the church up into pairs and went and knocked on all the doors of the houses, and gave every woman we met a beautiful red rose. The church members returned full of stories of women bursting into tears of gratitude, and many opportunities to pray. On Father's Day we did the same and gave out bars of chocolate to all the dads we met. On Halloween we threw a party for all the children on the estate called the 'Hallo Wayne Party'. The challenge was to discover who Wayne was (one of the church leaders dressed up!) and it was a wonderful party enjoyed by all. We gave out cream eggs at Easter and offered help and general information to new residents.

I really enjoyed living there, and always looked for ways to share my faith. Every summer I organised a barbecue in my garden and invited all my neighbours. It was such a fun time and such a good opportunity to get to know them. However, there was always one family who didn't attend and this left me feeling frustrated.

'How can I get to know them and encourage them to come to the barbecue?' I pondered. 'They're the only ones that don't come. What can I do, Lord?'

I decided to buy a pretty houseplant for the wife, and my idea was go and deliver it, introduce myself and invite her and the family to the barbecue. I prayed and asked God to bless this meeting.

I shut my front door behind me with the plant in my hands and walked down the road to their house. I went through the wooden gate, my heart beating a little faster than usual.

'I hope this works out,' I thought to myself. 'I so want to get to know them.'

I rang the doorbell and waited. Now my heart felt like it had jumped into my throat, and I was hoping it wouldn't ruin my well-prepared speech. A few moments went by, and no one came to answer the door, so I rang again, more than once this time, just to make sure they could hear.

Still no answer and I realised no one was home. My heart sank and I wandered out of the gate in the direction of my house. I looked at the plant in my hands. It was a begonia with fragrant, pink flowers. I lifted the plant close to my face and smelled the petals.

'Mmm, this is nice, this plant. Maybe I could just keep it for myself? No!' I chided. 'That's not what I bought it for. Tomorrow I'll try again.'

The next day I returned to my neighbour's house, a little later this time, in the hope that someone would be home. I rang the doorbell and moments later a middle-aged man, dressed in tracksuit bottoms and a T-shirt, answered the door.

'Oh, hi!' I exclaimed, a little surprised that at last someone was there. 'My name's Cally and I'm your neighbour. I live just a few doors up. Is your wife home?'

The man paused, looked a little crestfallen and replied, 'Um, no, er . . . I'm divorced. I live here with my son.'

'Oh no,' I thought to myself. 'Here I am with a plant for his wife, and he doesn't have a wife any more. Now what do I do?'

Wanting a hole to appear in front of me into which I could quickly disappear I replied hastily, 'Oh, well, er . . . sorry – um . . . I just wanted to invite you to the barbecue at my house next week. It's for all the neighbours in our road and it would be so nice if you could come. Here's the invitation and um . . . well, here's the plant too!' I thrust the invitation and the plant into his hands, feeling my face redden. 'It was so nice to meet you,' I said. I faced the direction of the gate and began to walk down the path.

I then heard him say, 'How beautiful, how beautiful, thank you so much.'

I turned around and saw him gazing at the flowers and then he lifted his head, smiling and waving goodbye.

'Bye! Hope to see you next week,' I called, and rushed off up the road to my house. I arrived out of breath and paused on the doorstep.

'Wow, that didn't go quite how I'd planned,' I said to myself, 'but he seemed to like the plant. Lord, please bring him to the barbecue!'

The following week my neighbours came to my house for the barbecue. All of them came, including my newfound neighbour and his son. I was overjoyed and so blessed that at last he had accepted the invitation.

Maybe a plant wasn't what I would have chosen to touch that man's heart, but God used it anyway. Sometimes just a small action or act of love can unlock someone's life, and even when we think we've got it wrong, God will use our act of obedience. We just need to step out in faith. Try it and see what happens!

I have a wonderful story that I heard during my time in Bosnia. I met a young American missionary working there and she told me this amazing story. I am including it in this chapter about 'getting it wrong' as it is such a good example of how perfectly God can use our mistakes.

A few years after working in Bosnia she went to the USA for a few months and left her small team in charge. Most of the team members had recently arrived in Mostar and were young and quite inexperienced so she left clear instructions of who to visit and how to help. Two of the young people responsible for the home visits were given the list of families and one afternoon they set off to visit the first name on the list. They were a bit nervous at the prospect of speaking the Bosnian language and trying to evangelise, but prayed before they left and asked God to help them.

Arriving at the first house on the list, they rang the doorbell and a middle-aged lady peered from behind the door. She was frail and thin and dressed in a housecoat and slippers. They noticed she was a bit cautious, but this was normal because of the war. The Bosnian people were still wary even of their neighbours, and she was obviously suspicious of these two strangers on her doorstep.

One of the young American missionaries cleared his throat, took a deep breath, looked down at his list and in the best Bosnian language he could muster, said, 'Good afternoon. We're from the church and we're visiting families registered with our project.' He then asked if the first person on his list lived there.

The lady looked confused and answered him quickly, 'I don't know God!'

Taken aback, the young man and his friend looked at each other in surprise and his colleague said with great enthusiasm, 'Well, that's what we're here for. Could we come in and have a chat?'

The lady was a little surprised but asked them in and the two young missionaries followed her into the lounge, still a little shocked at how easily this was going. The lady called her daughters and son, as she thought they would also like to meet the two young visitors. The two missionaries removed their coats and perched on the edge of the sofa. An hour later the lady, her teenage daughters and young son had all prayed and asked Jesus to be their Lord and Saviour!

They chatted for a while and were about to leave when she asked them to return that evening. She wanted them to meet her husband and neighbours too.

The young missionaries agreed enthusiastically and stood up to put on their coats. Just as they were going, one of them turned and paused, a little embarrassed, and said, 'I hope you don't mind me asking . . . When we asked you if the person on our list lived here why did you answer, "I don't know God"?'

The lady frowned, thought for a moment and then a huge smile spread across her lips.

'Oh!' she exclaimed. 'I think you must have misunderstood me. I have never heard of the person you asked about, so I replied, "God, I don't know!" You must have mixed up the words and thought I said, "I don't know God!"'

Apparently the two missionaries looked at each other and roared with laughter. The lady, her son and daughters also laughed in delight as they all realised the mistake that had been made. They hugged each other goodbye, and the couple promised to return that evening. The whole family became Christians that night, including several neighbours and friends.

Isn't that a great story? It's so wonderful how God uses our mistakes, our weaknesses and our blunders. All He requires is our obedience, and then He does the rest!

Questions

1. Have you ever 'got it wrong', trying to witness to someone or show them God's love? What happened? What would you do differently now?

2. Do you have a neighbour/friend/work colleague/family member who you could invite to a church service or event? Start to pray about them now.

3. Think of something you could do to show God's love to a member of your family/work colleague/ fellow student.

4. Think of something you could do to show God's love to a neighbour.

5. If someone said to you, 'I don't know God!', what would you say to them?

6. What does stepping out in faith look like for you? What gifts has God given you that you could use to bless others?

Click on the QR code to watch the video about this chapter

Forgiving and Receiving Forgiveness

> It is ultimately in our own best interest that we
> become forgiving, repentant, reconciling and
> reconciled people, because without forgiveness,
> without reconciliation we have no future[12]

The young boy's eyes twinkled, and a broad smile spread across his face.

'Next time you go to England, would you take me with you?' he joked, a hint of irony in his voice. 'How could I possibly take this boy to England with me when he's in prison here in Brazil?' I thought to myself.

'What's the food like there? And is it true it rains all the time? And what about The Beatles? Have you ever met them?'

His questions followed one after the other almost without pausing for breath and something drew me to this young man, so bright and curious.

'I'm so sorry, I have to leave now,' I said. 'It was really good to meet you and maybe I'll see you again soon.'

I hugged him goodbye and left the courtyard area where we had been talking to the boys. A heavy metal gate slid open to allow me through, and with a loud clang, closed behind me. Then another gate opened in front of me, and I walked into

---

12. Desmond Tutu, *No Future Without Forgiveness* (London: Rider, 1999).

an area flanked by offices with staff and guards working and chatting.

'Did you see that boy talking to me just then?' I asked Barbara, the director of the youth prison unit. 'What's his name?'

'Oh, that's Matheus,' she replied softly. 'Why do you ask?'

'He just seems such a nice lad, so friendly and intelligent.'

'Yes, he is. He's a lovely lad, but his story is so tragic,' she replied hurriedly, as if she wanted me to know. She took a deep breath. 'He was just thirteen years old when his mother committed suicide. She threw alcohol all over her body and set fire to herself in front of him. He did everything he could to try to save her, but she died in his arms.'

'Oh no.' I struggled to take in this awful news.

'After that, he went off the rails. He got involved with drugs and soon started drug trafficking. Then a few months later the traffickers in the *favela* where he lived recruited him as the debt collector.'

'The debt collector?' I asked. 'What do you mean?'

'His job was to collect the money from those who owed the drug traffickers.' She paused, took another deep breath and continued in a half-whisper. 'When they couldn't pay, he murdered them.'

'What? That's crazy,' I replied, trying to control my emotions and not raise my voice for everyone to hear. 'He started murdering people at thirteen?' I paused, not wanting to ask the next question. 'How many did he murder?'

'About twenty,' she replied, 'until he was brought here.' Barbara's expression was tense, and I knew this was just one story of one boy. As director of the youth prison, she knew many similar stories of desperate situations and it was obvious she cared deeply about each one of the boys in the unit. 'I have some news you'll be pleased to hear, though,' she said quickly, a smile breaking the sad expression on her face.

My mind was reeling as I tried not to think about the things I had just heard. I certainly needed some good news and wondered what she was going to say.

'Matheus became a Christian here a few months ago and is really transformed. He smiles and laughs now, very different from when he arrived.'

My heart was aching for this boy who I had just met but didn't know. I felt a wave of something rising inside me. I didn't know if it was love or grace or compassion, or maybe something else. I just knew I couldn't go home without talking to him again.

'Barbara, I'm so sorry, but is there any chance I could speak to him again, now, before we leave?'

'Of course,' she replied. 'Let me go and call him.' She stopped and turned around. 'Oh, but don't tell him what I told you, OK?'

'No, I won't,' I answered, a little disappointed. I was hoping to tell him that I knew a little of his story and that I wanted to help him.

She turned to go back through the sliding gate and as the bars clanked past her face, she stopped again, looked at me over her shoulder and said, 'No, it's OK, you can tell him you know.'

I watched her walk back into the courtyard and call Matheus. He came running to her side, and walked alongside her, stumbling a little as he tried to keep pace. He was dressed in the standard youth prison uniform of navy-blue shorts, a white T-shirt and flip flops. His clothes were branded with his identification number in the prison. The clothes were faded and old and I wondered how many other boys had worn those clothes and been given that number.

I took a few deep breaths and prayed, 'Lord, I need Your help. Please give me the words to say to this young boy, words that he needs to hear.'

A few moments later, the two of them arrived and Barbara left us alone in the middle of the corridor. Matheus seemed pleased to be able to talk a little more. I took both of his hands in mine and paused. I looked into his bright, twinkling eyes and opened my mouth, hoping God would fill it.

'Matheus, I asked Barbara if I could speak to you again. She told me a little bit about your story, and I couldn't go home without telling you ...' I took a deep breath, trying to stop my hands from shaking. 'I want you to know that Jesus loves you so much.'

Matheus gulped, looking straight into my eyes.

'Your past is in the past and you have a new life to live. God has wonderful plans for your life, Matheus.'

As I said the words, I felt an overwhelming love for this boy. It seemed to surge through me, and I could almost feel my heart wanting to explode. He looked at me, his eyes open wide, and I heard myself say, 'Could I give you a hug, Matheus? As a mum?'

Matheus thrust out his hands in front of him. 'Yes, please!' he cried, and threw his arms around me. I hugged him tightly, really tightly, whispering into his ear, 'Jesus loves you ... He loves you ... He loves you so much, Matheus.'

I felt his chest heave as he breathed in deeply, sobbing on my shoulder. We stood together in that embrace, oblivious of what was around us for maybe as much as a minute. After a while I began to loosen my grasp, but he held me tighter, as if he never wanted me to let him go, as if years of pain and grief and death were wrapped up in that one short embrace.

After what seemed like an eternity, we stepped back a little and looked at each other, tears rolling down our cheeks, our faces red and our brows wet with perspiration. Matheus smiled at me, his eyes twinkling more than ever, tears spilling over and running down his face.

'Matheus, I want to help you. When you leave here, please keep in touch. If you need anything I'm here for you, OK?'

'Thank you,' he replied, his eyes shining, and wiping his cheek with the back of his hand. 'Thank you so much,' he said again.

I left the youth prison and drove home. It felt like Matheus was glued to the forefront of my mind for the whole week afterwards. Everywhere I went and everything I did, I thought of him. The following week I returned to the youth prison, this time with two friends who were interested in helping develop the project.

'Good morning, Barbara,' I said. 'This is Karina, and this is André. Thank you so much for allowing them to visit.' They shook Barbara's hand, and she welcomed them to the youth prison. 'Would it be OK if I introduce them to Matheus?' I asked.

'Of course,' Barbara replied. 'Why don't you wait in that room over there and I'll call him?'

We entered a small classroom, pulled four chairs into the centre of the room, and sat down to wait. The classroom was empty except for about fifteen chairs and a small white plastic table. The walls were bare and grey. There was a chalkboard on one side and the room was half-lit with one light bulb hanging from the ceiling. The windows were at the top of the walls, long, narrow, horizontal panes of glass with bars in front of them to prevent any possible escape.

'Not even Spider-Man would be able to get out of here,' I thought to myself. The windows were slanted open, allowing a small space for air to come in and I was grateful for some relief from the stifling heat.

Matheus appeared at the door, and I rushed over to give him a big hug.

'Hi, Matheus! Thank you, Barbara, is it OK if we chat to him?'

'Yes,' she replied. 'Just give us a call when you've finished.'

'Thank you,' I answered, and with Matheus by my side we returned to the centre of the room.

'These are my friends, Matheus, and they're very pleased they could come and meet you today. This is Karina. She's a businesswoman, and she helps with charities like ours.'

'Nice to meet you, Matheus,' Karina said, gesturing for him to sit down. She was very experienced with charity work, but this was her first time at the youth prison.

'And this is my friend André, he's a businessman,' she added, 'and he's helping Cally and the project too.'

'I'm really happy to meet you, Matheus,' André said, greeting him with the typical Brazilian young people's handshake. This involves pulling your hand back as if stroking the other person's hand and then doing a little punch onto the other person's fist. 'This is our first time at the youth prison and it's really good to be able to find out more about the project, and especially to meet you.'

'I haven't told them anything about you, Matheus,' I said, 'except that you're a lovely lad and that you're very funny and intelligent!' We all laughed, breaking the tension a little, and I continued, 'I wonder, would you mind telling us a bit of your story?'

'Yes, that's fine,' Matheus replied, taking a long deep breath and leaning forward in his chair. 'I have done many things wrong,' he said slowly, choosing his words carefully, 'and I realise now just what a bad person I was. It all began when my mum committed suicide. I was just thirteen and I didn't know what to do. I felt so angry and so desperate and had no one to talk to.' He took a deep breath and continued, his voice cracking slightly as he spoke. 'I always talked to my mum when I had problems. I was really close to her, the closest of all of us. Suddenly she wasn't there any more, and I really didn't have anyone to look after me. I went to live with my grandma after my mum died, but she was grieving too for my mum, and I didn't have anyone to talk to.

'I realise now I desperately wanted to forget about my pain, and I got involved in all sorts of wrong things. I was only thirteen but suddenly I was getting recognition for all the bad things I was doing, and it felt good. But then I began to work as the debt collector, and it all went wrong.' He paused for a few seconds, and then continued, 'So wrong. I did so many wrong things.' At this moment Matheus' shoulders began to shake and big tears began to well up in his eyes. 'I did so many things wrong,' he repeated. He looked down and tears started to fall at such a rate that they began to form a small pool of water on the floor in front of him. He cried like that for a few minutes. I looked at Karina and André and they too were weeping and wiping their eyes.

After a few moments, André stood up and pulled his chair alongside Matheus. He was a tall man and as he placed his arm around his shoulder, Matheus laid his head gently on his upper arm.

'Thank you for sharing your story with us, Matheus,' he said gently. 'That must have taken a lot of courage.'

Matheus, his face a bleary mess of snot and tears, wiped his face on his sleeve.

'Then one day I went to a meeting held by a local church. They came here one Sunday and told us about forgiveness. I prayed and asked God to forgive me for all those terrible things I did, and I understood for the first time that Jesus died on the cross so I could be forgiven. I also understood that I needed to forgive myself, but that's a process I'm still going through.' He stopped and smiled. 'I felt so different after I prayed that day, like a huge weight had lifted off my shoulders.

'God has changed my life and when I leave here, I'm going to live with my brother in Rio de Janeiro. I don't want to go back to the *favela* where I lived with my mum. There are too many memories there and too many old friends. I'll have a brand-new start in Rio and my dream is to go to university. My brother's married and working, and I know I'll be fine there.'

'That sounds like a great idea,' Karina said, 'and you can keep in touch with Cally and The Eagle Project and let us know how you're doing.'

'I'd like that,' he replied. 'Thank you so much for coming to visit me.'

When Matheus was released a few months later,[13] he returned to Rio de Janeiro to live with his brother as planned. I phoned a short time afterwards and discovered that he was at university and doing very well. I don't know how he is today as we lost contact after his mobile phone number changed. However, I have never forgotten him, and pray he is continuing to walk with God, living in the truth of the grace and forgiveness he so desperately needs to know.

Questions

1. What did you think when you read this chapter?

2. Why and how is God's forgiveness available to us?

3. Matheus described a feeling of a weight being lifted off his shoulders when he received God's forgiveness. Have you ever experienced that?

4. When we forgive someone, it is a decision, not an emotion. Reflect on what that means for you, right now, in your life.

5. Is there someone you need to forgive? How can you release forgiveness to that person?

6. Would you consider serving God in a prison ministry? Think about this.

---

13. Adolescents in Brazil serve a maximum prison sentence of three years.

Click on the QR code to watch the video about this chapter

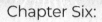

Chapter Six:

A Link in the Chain

So neither the one who plants no the one who waters is
anything, but only God, who makes things grow. The one
who plants and the one who waters have one purpose,
and they will each be rewarded according to their own
labour. For we are fellow workers in God's service;
you are God's field, God's building.

(1 Corinthians 3:7-9)

It was rush hour and the evening train from London was standing room only. I was grateful to be almost home, and a few moments later arrived at Milton Keynes railway station. I walked through the automatic doors and the cold winter air bit into my cheeks. I pulled my scarf tighter around my neck.

'Wow, what a lot of taxis,' I thought. There was a long line of black cabs waiting alongside the pavement, moving very slowly as they picked up the passengers who had left the train before me. A cab stopped by my side, and I jumped in, grateful to be out of the cold and wind.

'Good evening, how are you?' I asked.

'I am very well,' the taxi driver answered, 'and where are you going this evening?'

He was an elderly man with a strong Indian accent. Instantly I warmed to his friendly manner as I remembered with fondness my time in India.

I gave him my destination, and settled back into my seat.

'I'm quite shocked at how many taxis were waiting at the station,' I said as we drove off. 'I don't use the train much and was really surprised to see so many.'

'Yes, it is very difficult,' the taxi driver replied. 'Sometimes we have to wait for hours just to get one customer.'

'That must be really hard,' I replied, 'and there are no cafés or restaurants at the station for you to buy something to eat or drink?'

'No, sometimes my tummy rumbles a lot,' he answered, and we both laughed out loud. 'And it would be so good to have a nice hot drink in this cold winter weather.'

Soon my trip was over, and I thanked him for the journey and climbed out of the taxi. I unlocked my front door, pulled off my winter coat and scarf and plumped down on my sofa.

'Nothing to eat or drink,' I thought. 'Hours waiting for a customer? Could we do something to help them?'

The next evening, I contacted my house group leader, Trevor Clift. He was a lovely man with a huge heart for people (he sadly died several years ago) and was always very involved in the evangelistic events that the church organised.

'Trev, I've been thinking,' I said enthusiastically. 'Do you think we could bless the taxi drivers at the train station? I travelled back from London last night and when I arrived, there was a huge, long line of taxis just sitting there waiting. I asked my taxi driver and he said that sometimes they wait there for hours. He also said they have nowhere to get food or drink. So, could we go there once a week, on Friday nights, maybe, and take flasks of coffee and tea and even some snacks? It would be such a cool way of blessing them. Most of them are Indian or Pakistani so they are probably Muslims or Hindus, and we can show them Jesus' love in a practical way!'

'I like this idea, Cally,' Trevor replied quickly. 'I'll talk to Danny and see what he thinks.' Danny was our pastor and a very warm-hearted man with a real desire to reach out in all different ways. I had a feeling he was going to like the idea too!

The following Friday evening we met at Trevor's house to pray, and then set out. There was Trevor, me and a couple of other volunteers from the church. Armed with our flasks, cups, spoons, sugar and biscuits, we arrived at the station and approached the first taxi in the queue. The driver was a bit surprised to see us standing beside his window, but rolled it down and we all said, 'Hi.' He was a middle-aged Indian man with a big friendly smile and a long grey beard.

'Good evening, my name's Trevor, and we're from the local church,' Trevor said, in his lovely, friendly way. 'We thought it would be nice to offer you some hot drinks to warm you up a bit in this cold wintry weather. We have tea or coffee, whichever you prefer.'

'Oh, oh, my goodness, that is very, very kind,' the taxi driver replied. 'Yes, please, I would love a cup of tea. Two sugars, please. How long have you been doing this?'

'We just started tonight,' Trevor replied. 'And you're our first customer!'

'Oh, well, I am very grateful. Thank you so much. Um . . . how much is it, please?'

'Oh, it's free!' I exclaimed. 'You don't need to pay. We're just here to bless you.'

The man took the cup of tea and a biscuit, his hands trembling in the cold.

'Well, that is really something. Thank you very much,' he said, obviously touched by our actions. The driver in the queue behind him was so curious he left his taxi with the engine running and came to see what was happening. He also accepted a cup of tea.

We continued along the line of taxis, introducing ourselves and pouring out hot drinks, asking them their names and chatting about life in general. Only a few refused the drinks and shut their car windows up, obviously not wanting to talk. We discovered later that some of them were wary of our actions at first, suspicious that we might be a rival taxi firm and thinking we had put laxatives in the coffee and tea! A few weeks later, when they realised we were genuine, they were more than happy to accept the blessing.

That was the beginning of our ministry to the taxi drivers that continued for many years in Milton Keynes and was even adopted by other churches. Every Friday we went to the train station, rain or shine, snow or ice – whatever the weather, we were there.

We had some amazing conversations about our faith, and prayed with many of the cab drivers on different occasions. Even today they still remember what we did. On a recent visit to Milton Keynes, I met an old friend from my church who told me that he lives in the same cul-de-sac as one of the taxi drivers, a Muslim man who always mentions us and told him that he had given his life to Jesus.

However, one very special thing happened there at that station. One of the taxi drivers was very friendly; his name was Clive. He always stopped to chat to us, and we got to know him quite well over the months. He was a middle-aged man with a family, and we always made a point of asking how they were.

One Friday evening he pulled up alongside us and rolled down his window. We all greeted him, and I continued chatting to him while the rest of the team moved along to the next taxi.

'How's life?' I asked.

I certainly wasn't expecting his reply.

'I'm fine, thanks, but I need your help, Cally,' he said, with concern in his voice. 'My son just sits in his bedroom all the time and hardly ever comes downstairs. He just sits up there reading the Bible, and then comes down to the living room and asks me a whole load of questions! Cally, I don't know anything about the Bible. I can't answer him. What do you advise me to do?'

Well, this was a lovely surprise. That was a question I was very happy to be asked. I could see our taxi ministry wasn't in vain.

'Wow, Clive, that's so good that he's interested in the Bible and obviously seeking God,' I replied enthusiastically. 'My suggestion is that he does an Alpha course.[14] My church offers the course, and it's free and aimed at people just like your son who have questions about God. It's really relaxed, and it will be a good opportunity for him to get out of the house and make some new friends. What do you think?'

'That sounds great, Cally, thanks,' Clive replied, with an expression of relief on his face. 'How can I get him signed up?'

'Here is the phone number to contact,' I answered, handing him a business card that had the church details on the front and written on the back:

This act of love is to let you know that Jesus loves you
and you are important to Him!

We used these cards in all our acts of evangelism in Milton Keynes and they were very useful, especially at moments like this.

'Oh, thank you so much, Cally,' Clive replied. 'I'll talk to him as soon as I get home.'

'You're so welcome, and don't worry, at Alpha he will receive the help he needs.'

A customer arrived and jumped into Clive's taxi, and he sped off, waving out of the window. I was so overjoyed and ran to tell the rest of the team.

---

14. See https://alpha.org.uk (accessed 6 January 2023).

'You guys are not going to believe what just happened! Clive told me he has a problem. His son just sits in his bedroom all the time reading the Bible, and then asks Clive questions he doesn't know how to answer! He asked what he should do? How cool is that? I told him to get him signed up at our church for the Alpha course.'

The team were so overjoyed, and we joined hands and prayed for Clive's son right at that moment. I didn't see Clive for a few weeks and then out of the blue, his taxi appeared and drew alongside me.

'Hey, Clive, good to see you. How's your son doing? Did he start the Alpha course?' I asked expectantly.

'Hi, Cally, good to see you too. Yes, thank you so much. My son is doing the Alpha course and is loving it and has stopped asking me difficult questions! He's very different from how he was a few weeks ago. He's getting out more and has made some new friends. I'm so grateful for your help.'

We chatted some more, and I discovered that his son was in fact doing the Alpha course at another church near his home, not at my church. That was absolutely fine with me. It isn't about counting numbers and me winning points. The most important thing is being a link in the chain for someone to find salvation.

'That's such good news, Clive. Maybe you should do the Alpha course too – get some answers to those difficult questions!' I replied cheekily.

'Yes, I've actually been thinking about doing that,' Clive answered.

I was so blessed that God was obviously at work in this family and hoped Clive would get round to doing the Alpha course too.

Several weeks went by and we didn't see Clive on our Friday evening visits to the station. One Sunday morning I was getting ready for church and the phone rang. It was Dave

Eyeington, one of the leaders of the church who was part of the train station team.

'Hi, Cally, how are you doing?' he asked.

'Good, thanks, Dave, how are you?' I replied.

'I'm well, thanks, but I have some sad news for you.' He paused. 'Actually, some sad news and some good news.'

I had no idea what Dave was about to say. Firstly, I wasn't expecting a phone call from Dave on a Sunday morning, but also was confused about the good and bad news.

'Cally, I'm so sorry to tell you this but Clive, our taxi-driver friend, was killed in a car accident recently.'

'No!' I cried. 'Not Clive? Oh no, what happened? How did you find out?'

'I just saw the front of the local newspaper,' Dave replied. 'There's an article all about the accident. He was involved in a crash caused by another driver and his car was crushed by a lorry.'

I sat down heavily on the chair beside me, so sad to hear this tragic news.

'There is some good news though, Cally,' Dave quickly added. I couldn't think of any good news in this awful situation, but Dave continued, 'In the article it says that four weeks earlier he had become a born-again Christian.'

I gasped. Dave read from the paper, how Clive was a popular man who changed when he became a Christian, and how his faith had helped him.

'He became a Christian, Cally, a month before he died! Isn't that wonderful?' Dave exclaimed.

'Dave! I'm in shock. That's amazing. Obviously, I'm so sad he died, but so glad he died a Christian!'

My mind was reeling. 'How did that happen?' I wondered. 'I knew his son did the Alpha course, but did he become a Christian and then take his dad to church? Did Clive do the

Alpha course? What? How, Lord?' So many questions filled my mind as I tried to work out what had happened.

Details didn't really matter that day and still don't today. What mattered was that Clive knew Jesus before he died and today, he is with God. What a wonderful end to such a tragic accident. Our station taxi-driver team was certainly part of the blessing, a link in the chain that helped him find Christ.

When we witness to someone about our faith in Jesus Christ, there may be others who witnessed before us and others who will follow. We are simply one of the links in the chain. What a privilege to know that we can be part of a chain that will set someone free for all of eternity.

I love this story, although obviously I am sad that Clive died. It encourages me to be creative in my outreach, to look for new ways to bless, and to believe that the seed we sow will bear fruit. I look forward to meeting Clive in heaven, and his son, and hopefully many of the other taxi drivers too!

Questions

These questions are a little bit different! Get a notebook, or large sheet of paper, and think about these individually or with others:

1. Consider special dates in the year like Christmas and Easter. What different events could your church do at these times?

2. Could you start or help start an ongoing activity or initiative – a food bank, for example?

3. Who are the people groups in your town or community? How could you bless them?

4. Think about different age groups – babies, children, adolescents, youth, adults, the elderly.

Reflect on what you have written, and pray. Also pray for an opportunity to share your ideas with a church leader. Ask God to help you pray with like-minded others, and to show you which ideas to pursue.

Click on the QR code to watch the video about this chapter

Chapter Seven:

Be Expectant that God Will Answer

Let us then approach God's throne of grace with
confidence, so that we may receive mercy and
find grace to help us in our time of need.

(Hebrews 4:16)

When God answers your prayers, is your first reaction one of surprise? That's strange, isn't it? We pray and have faith that God will hear us and then when He does, we're shocked that He answered!

I am still learning to trust Him more. I know my faith has grown stronger and deeper during these last thirty-two years of walking with God, and I am learning not to be so surprised any more.

A few years ago, I became very ill here in São Paulo, with double pneumonia. I was at home alone, feeling very unwell indeed. Halfway through the morning I woke up in a pool of perspiration and realised I needed to drink some water. I stumbled into the bathroom and looked in the mirror. My face was pale, and my eyes were puffy and red. My chest ached from all the coughing, and I felt like my legs were going to buckle beneath me. I also realised I needed to eat something but knew I didn't have the strength to cook.

'Father, please help me,' I prayed weakly. 'I need some soup. Please send me some soup to help me feel better.'

I had no idea how God was going to give me this soup. Nowadays I could consult various restaurants online and ask for it to be delivered, but in those days deliveries like that didn't exist. I walked slowly and carefully downstairs to get some water, aware that at any moment my legs could give way. Before reaching the kitchen, I collapsed on the sofa in a heap and lay there for a few minutes, almost dozing off before beginning yet another coughing fit.

I came to my senses as I heard a car horn beeping in the road outside my house.

'Who could that be?' I thought, not expecting it to be for me.

Then I heard the doorbell ring at the same time as the car horn.

'Maybe it is for me,' I thought, and then panicked as I realised I looked dreadful, with my hair unbrushed and with no make-up. (That might not seem relevant to you, but I am very blonde, and my eyebrows and eyelashes are white, so I avoid meeting people without my make-up on, even in the most extreme of circumstances!)

I fumbled as I tried to unlock the front door and made my way slowly to the gate.

'Coming!' I tried to shout, worried the person might have already left and at the same time, hoping they had.

I opened the gate to see Mary Fawcett, my dear American friend, known to all as Aunt Mary, a missionary and pastor's wife in Brazil for many years. As always, she was looking lovely, her hair beautifully styled and wearing make-up and dark-red lipstick. I remembered how awful I was looking and opened my mouth to apologise.

'Hello, dear Cally,' she said before I could speak. 'Oh, my goodness, you don't look well at all. I've brought you some things to help you feel better.'

I tried to explain that I looked awful because of my lack of make-up, but she bustled through the gate and closed it behind her. She took my arm and gently led me back into the house, balancing a big basket in her other arm as she walked alongside me.

I sat weakly on a chair as she began to unpack the basket.

'I heard you were sick, Cally, so now you need the right food to help you get well.'

Mary removed her coat and placed it on the sofa. She then began to unpack the basket and hold up one by one all the different items inside.

'Here, I brought some pineapple juice – it's good for releasing catarrh, and this is banana bread, my special recipe. Here is some wholemeal bread and these are some homemade cookies, and this is ...' She held up a large flask and declared, 'And this is what you really need – some delicious homemade soup!'

I stared at Aunt Mary, not sure if I was seeing her in person or an angel. Tears of gratitude began to well up in my eyes.

'Mary, I just prayed, literally minutes ago, and asked God to send me some soup. I knew I wouldn't feel well enough to cook, and I just prayed, "Father, please send me some soup." Now you've arrived not only with soup but with so many other wonderful goodies to go with it. Thank you, Mary, thank you so much for being open to the Holy Spirit's touch. You truly are amazing.'

God's prods – that's what I like to call them, when we get a prod from the Holy Spirit, nudging us to contact someone, to help them or take them something they need. Wow – that day was so special; I felt so loved by God and so very grateful for Mary's love and care. I prayed a specific prayer and God answered in a very specific way. It makes the miracle even greater, doesn't it, when we pray that way?

Dear Aunt Mary passed into Jesus' arms last year, from COVID-19, and I shared this story at her memorial service. I wanted her family to know, as I was sure she hadn't told them.

This was one of those secret acts of love and kindness that she often did, that only the recipients knew about.

I love to reflect on the timing of these moments. I prayed the prayer a few moments before Aunt Mary arrived. However, the Holy Spirit had already nudged her hours before I had even prayed. It took a while to prepare that soup, make the bread, the cookies, and get everything together. Isn't that wonderful? God's timing is beyond our understanding. These precious moments move us closer to God and remind us of just how faithfully He watches over us.

I had a similar experience during a visit to the UK in 2020 when I was invited to speak about my first book on TBN, the Christian TV channel in London. The whole country was in lockdown, so I was staying in an Airbnb which I found through a Facebook group for Brazilians living in the UK.

I had been staying with a very kind lady who had offered me her spare room, but when her friend needed somewhere to stay, I had to move on. However, in the middle of lockdown, it was impossible to find anywhere to live!

All the hotels were closed except for frontline workers and all my friends were respecting the COVID-19 rules so I couldn't invade their 'bubbles'. I remember walking out of a train station having just discovered I had nowhere to stay, and feeling shellshocked.

What was I going to do? Where was I going to stay? I felt like a foreigner in my own land. It was a freezing cold afternoon, and I began to imagine myself shivering under a bridge that night, sleeping on the streets along with the other unfortunate street-dwellers.

I was dressed smartly in a winter coat and scarf so was quite surprised when suddenly a thin man with long, tangled grey hair appeared out of nowhere and said in a rather slurred voice, 'Are...you...homeless?'

'Um . . . kind of, yes!' I answered quickly, not really knowing what to say.

'What?' I thought to myself. 'Do I look homeless?' I was very confused. 'Oh Lord – has a spirit of homelessness come upon me?' I asked myself, almost in tears. 'Why is this man asking me that?'

'Do you want to come back to my place for a coffee?' he asked, now obviously more interested in my plight, and leering at me with a drunken smile. He was shabbily dressed in an old overcoat and dirty boots.

'No!' I replied, stepping backwards and speaking a little more loudly than was polite. 'I mean, no, thank you, I'm just fine . . . uh . . . thank you, bye,' and I rushed down the road, hoping he wouldn't follow me.

A few hundred metres ahead I stopped and leaned against a wall, slightly out of breath from walking so fast, my cheeks and eyes stinging in the biting cold wind.

'That was a bit crazy, but what am I going to do now?' I wondered, and then suddenly remembered the Brazilian Facebook group. I hurriedly typed a message asking if anyone knew of an Airbnb, and almost immediately received a message from Cristina, who replied in Portuguese telling me of an Airbnb very close by.

'Wow, thank you so much,' I said when I arrived a few minutes later and Cristina showed me to my flat. 'You don't know how relieved I am to have found this place.'

A few moments later I was almost crying again, but this time from laughing so hard as I told her of my strange encounter with the man asking me if I was homeless, which in fact I was.

'Cally, I'm so glad you are here. I can't imagine what could have happened to you,' she said, giving me a huge hug. She was typically Brazilian with long dark-brown hair, and very warm and friendly. She introduced me to the two other families living in the building, both from Brazil, having recently moved to the UK. I instantly felt at home and over the next few days got to know them well, sharing delicious cups of Brazilian coffee and making the most of being able to speak in Portuguese.

Later that week I went down with COVID-19 and was fine apart from a cough, mild cold symptoms, pain in my back and legs and absolutely no sense of smell. Various friends from Brazil and the UK phoned me, extremely concerned for my well-being and telling me to keep warm and rest. That was easy. I couldn't go anywhere, and the Airbnb was lovely and warm, with radiators piping hot to keep me from feeling the cold of the winter weather outside.

Cristina and the two Brazilian families did my food shopping, brought me soup and goodies to eat, leaving everything outside my door with notes of encouragement and flowers. Isn't that special? Still today I reflect on how God called me to Brazil and then sent Brazilians to help me in my own country. Awesome!

It was all going smoothly until one morning, day six of COVID, when I woke up to a freezing cold bedroom and the radiator like a block of ice. My cough had worsened during the night, and I remembered everyone telling me that day six might be when I would get worse and need to be hospitalised!

'Oh no, why is this room so cold?' I thought, feeling a slight sense of panic as I wondered why the heating wasn't working. I grabbed my phone.

'Hi, Cris. It's so cold here in the flat,' I typed. 'The radiators aren't working and it's like a freezer in here.'

'I know,' she typed back. 'The family on the first floor have been awake all night, with the boiler making very strange noises. The boiler is in the corner of their bedroom, and they were terrified all night that it was going to explode.

'I've contacted the gas company,' she continued, 'but the bad news is they are on strike.'

On strike? My heart sank.

'Did they give you any idea of when they could send someone out?' I asked.

'They said the soonest they can come out is Thursday,' Cristina replied.

It was Monday. Would I survive three days in the freezing cold, with COVID?

'Sorry, I told them it's an emergency,' she apologised, 'but I don't know if anyone will come out before Thursday. I'll get back to you as soon as I have any news.'

I will be honest with you, I felt absolutely desolate. I was in a very unusual situation. In normal circumstances I would have phoned a friend or a hotel to stay somewhere else for a few nights, but I was ill with COVID-19! The country was in lockdown. I literally couldn't go anywhere.

I raced around the bedroom and hurriedly picked up my purse, laptop and documents. I stuffed them all into a large handbag and slung it across my shoulder.

If the boiler explodes and the roof is blown off, at least my documents and valuables will be attached to me, I reasoned, imagining the boiler exploding and me being ejected at high speed through the roof and into the garden below.

I decided that dressing in layers would be the best option, so put on a sweatshirt over my pyjamas, then my dressing gown and some warm, woolly socks. I gathered up the thick duvet from the bed and carried it into the living room. I wrapped myself in it, sat down on the sofa, pulled my handbag (still slung over my shoulder) to my side, and burst into tears.

'Lord, please help me,' I prayed. 'You know I have COVID, and I can't stay here in this cold. I don't want it to turn into pneumonia. Lord, I need You so much right now. Please do something to help me.'

I sat there for a few minutes, my sniffing breaking the silence, praying and asking God to intervene.

'Maybe some nice gas man will have pity on us and come and help,' I thought. At the same time, I knew the reality that if the company workers were on strike, then almost certainly no one would come before Thursday. I sat there for several minutes, wondering how I was going to avoid getting hypothermia. My nose was already freezing cold, and I pulled the duvet over my head in attempt to keep myself warm.

Suddenly a loud noise in the flat below broke the silence. It sounded like a huge roll of thunder, and I pulled my handbag closer to me, waiting for the roof to be blown off. I felt like my heart had stopped beating and I held my breath, waiting for the explosion.

Then I heard a loud click.

I waited.

I could now feel my heart beating in my throat. I exhaled quickly and took a deep breath. Was the boiler about to explode? Was I about to meet my Maker?

I strained to hear. A steady hum could be heard from the room below and I wondered what on earth was happening. Suddenly the living room radiator made a noise. It was the sound I was accustomed to hearing when the thermostat in the flat turned the heating on.

I jumped off the sofa and ran to the radiator, covering it with both my hands in anticipation. I stayed in that position for a few minutes, bent over the radiator, willing it to become warm. Very gradually a gentle heat began to penetrate my stone-cold fingers and I realised the boiler really had begun to work. I went back to the sofa and grabbed my phone.

'It's working, Cris, the boiler has come back on!' I shouted down the phone.

'I know, Cally,' she answered. 'I managed to mend it.'

'What? Cris? You mended the boiler? How did you do that?'

'I did a degree in Industrial Maintenance in Brazil,' she replied proudly. 'I accessed the boiler from my computer here and managed to get it working.'

'You are incredible, Cris!' I shouted in delight. 'Thank you so much! I think I might have died if I'd had to stay here with COVID for three days in the freezing cold.'

'Yes, I don't like to think what might have happened, Cally,' she laughed. 'Don't worry, everything should be fine now. Hope you feel better soon.'

For days afterwards I reflected on what had happened. Firstly, my shock that Cristina had a degree in Industrial Maintenance from a university in Brazil. I felt so sad for her and so many people around the world who move to other nations hoping to get work. However, the sad reality is that many end up working in menial jobs just to survive when in fact they are highly qualified in other areas.

I did feel extremely grateful, however, that I 'happened' to be staying in an Airbnb with someone who was qualified in Industrial Maintenance to look after me. We became great friends, and I was recently invited to translate at her wedding here in Brazil to Daniel, who is from the UK.

I also reflected on my sense of total powerlessness to change my situation. I could go nowhere and could do nothing to change my plight. I couldn't even walk out of the door of the Airbnb as I was ill with COVID-19, and the UK was in strict lockdown.

It was a deeply humbling experience of falling at God's feet and asking Him to rescue me. I prayed and He heard! Yet again He was so close by, taking care of everything, making sure I would be OK. Why would I be surprised?

Questions

1. Do you expect miraculous answers to prayer? Be honest!

2. Think about someone who has been an answer to prayer for you, and thank God for them.

3. Do you know anyone who is ill? Pray for that person.

4. Is there someone with practical needs where you live or work, or within your family? How could you *be* Jesus to that person?

5. The Brazilian women helped me when I had COVID-19. Are there people around you in your neighbourhood, workplace, school etc. from other nations who are new to the country? How could you do something practical to bless them?

6. What activities does your church do in order to reach out to the community? Could you get involved? Could you start something new?

Click on the QR code to watch the video about this chapter

Chapter Eight:

God's Prods!

I will hasten and not delay to obey your commands.
(Psalm 119:60)

In the last chapter I wrote about God's prods – about dear Aunt Mary responding to the Holy Spirit's prod to bring me soup and be the answer to my prayer. Have you ever felt God prod you to stop and pray for someone, show them God's love, or talk to them about Jesus? I want to encourage you to be ready for these God prods. If you are open to sharing your faith anywhere and at any moment, then be assured God will send His Holy Spirit to prod you!

My problem is that sometimes God needs to prod me more than once before I respond. Many years ago, when my sons were six and four years old, we went to visit a large park in São Paulo. It was a beautiful sunny day, and the park was full of families on bicycles, skateboards and rollerblades.

We had just gone through the main gates when my younger son, Joseph, stopped in his tracks and asked, 'Mum, before we rent the bikes, could we have a hot dog, please?' He had just spied the hot dog stand at the side of the park and looked up at me with that puppy dog expression of his that was almost impossible to resist.

I knew better than to suggest a long bike ride on an empty stomach so replied, 'OK, let's eat first, then, and after that we'll hire the bikes.' We wandered off in the direction of the hot dog stand and a few minutes later the boys were tucking into giant-size hot dogs with all the trimmings: mashed potato, ketchup and mayonnaise. I sat down at the table beside them, enjoying the warm weather and the atmosphere of the park.

We laughed as we watched several children descending helter-skelter down the slope in the direction of the bike hire station. Their mums and dads were chasing after them, screaming for them to slow down. I suddenly went into a cold sweat as I remembered the last time we came to this park.

It was a few months before and the time had come to return the bikes. The boys cycled ahead, making the most of the last few precious seconds, me pedalling as fast as my legs would go to keep up with them.

Before I knew it, Joseph was flying at breakneck speed down the final slope, shouting 'Whee!' at the top of his voice, oblivious of any danger he might be facing. I remember wondering, in horror, if this was to be my final glimpse of my son, alive and intact.

'Joseph!' I hollered at the top of my voice. 'Slow down!' I was watching as he used his feet to brake and holding my breath for what was about to happen. Fortunately, he was able to manage a wide curve, reducing his speed and coming to a dramatic halt in front of the bike station.

'Mum, do you remember last time?' Joseph broke my thoughts with a cheeky grin on his face.

'Yes, I do, Joe,' I replied seriously, and gave him that kind of 'mum' look that said, 'Don't even think of repeating that again, my son.'

I returned to watching the scene being played out before me. Families were enjoying ice cream cones and lollies, the ice cream melting fast and dripping down the children's chins. Dogs were barking and chasing each other, wagging their tails wildly in excitement. I could smell popcorn and hamburgers, potato chips and hot dogs. Teenagers wearing earphones flew past us at high speed on skateboards, seemingly oblivious of their surroundings.

Benjamin and Joseph were devouring the hot dogs, their noses and chins now decorated with ketchup and mayonnaise. I was seated with my back to where people were hiring rollerblades and despite all the noise of the park, I could hear a woman's voice chatting to her friend.

'My daughter is so unwell; I just don't know what to do,' she said, worriedly. 'She's lost so much weight and really has no appetite at all these days. Every time she eats, she has terrible stomach pain and feels nauseous or has diarrhoea. The doctor wants to operate but doesn't really know what is wrong with her. I am sick with worry – I just don't know what to do.'

I turned my head and saw a young girl slumped on a chair beside the rows of rollerblades. She was about fifteen and really didn't look well. Her hair was pulled back into a ponytail and it was obvious she was in pain. She was clutching her stomach and looked as if she was going to throw up. I could see her mum standing just behind her. She was middle-aged, with concern written all over her face.

'Go and pray for her!' a voice said in my head.

I knew it was a God prod but didn't want to obey.

'Oh, Lord,' I said. 'It's my day off and I'm with the boys . . . What if she doesn't want me to pray?' I added, now trying to make excuses.

'Go and ask if you can pray for her,' God said again.

'God! Really?' I replied, almost shouting inside my head.

There was silence.

I continued watching the scene before me and then began to feel a little uncomfortable. My face was beginning to feel very hot, and my heart was beating faster than usual. I tried to ignore what was happening but felt more and more like I was going to explode. I realised there was nothing for it. I needed to go and pray for this girl.

The boys had finished their hot dogs and were licking their lips and wiping their noses and chins with their sleeves.

'Boys, I just heard that lady over there saying her daughter is very ill,' I said, stuffing napkins into their hands and wiping Joe's face. 'Let's go and pray for her and ask Jesus to heal her, OK? Let's go.'

'OK, Mum,' the boys replied happily. They were used to me doing this kind of thing, and we all wandered over to the woman. I felt rather awkward, but the woman smiled, and obviously thought I was going to hire some skates.

'Hi,' I said. 'I hope you don't mind, but I just overheard your conversation about your daughter and . . . um . . . well, I'm a Christian and I really believe God can heal her and I wonder if you would like me to pray for your daughter?' The woman looked surprised, and I wasn't sure what she was going to say.

'Oh, yes, of course, yes, I would love you to pray for her,' she cried, a huge smile spreading across her face and her eyes lighting up with hope. 'I'm at my wits' end and I just don't know what to do any more.'

'What's your daughter's name?' I asked.

'Vanessa,' she replied.

I moved to stand beside her daughter and said, 'Is that OK with you, Vanessa? Can we ask Jesus to heal your tummy?'

Vanessa nodded and smiled. Ben and Joe stood beside me, and we all put our hands on her shoulders.

'Lord, thank You for Your healing power,' I prayed. 'We ask you to heal Vanessa and make her completely well. We pray for you to take away the pain, help her to eat normally again, and we pray that she won't need an operation. In Jesus' name. Amen.'

'Amen!' everyone agreed enthusiastically, and Vanessa's mum hugged me tight, tears rolling down her cheeks.

'Thank you, thank you, thank you,' she cried. 'I am so grateful; I'm sure she will be fine.'

It was such a short and simple prayer, nothing super-spiritual, but I believed God could heal her and was so grateful for the opportunity to pray for this young girl.

'We're just off to hire some bicycles now,' I explained, 'so take care and it was lovely to meet you.'

'It was so good to meet you too,' the woman replied, and hugged Ben and Joe tightly as she said goodbye. 'And if you ever want to hire some rollerblades I'll give you a discount,' she said.

We all laughed and thanked her for the offer, and the three of us wandered off in the direction of the bike hire station.

'Well, that was different,' I thought to myself. 'I thought we were coming to the park to hire bikes, not to pray for healing, but God, You gave me the prod, so I really pray she gets healed. She's in Your hands now!'

We had a wonderful afternoon, whizzing around the park on the bicycles, with an obligatory pause for ice cream and Guaraná, a typical Brazilian fizzy drink made with a berry from the Amazon. The return of the bikes went without a hitch this time, and we returned home, happy with our day at the park.

Vanessa stayed in my mind for the next few days, and I wondered how she was feeling and if her stomach was healed. I continued praying for her, that God would do a miracle in her life and that she and her mum would see His power at work.

About a month later we returned to the park to go for a bike ride again, and stopped at the rollerblade point on our way into the park. Vanessa's mum saw me from afar and came rushing up to talk to me.

'How's Vanessa?' I asked, eager to hear what her mother had to say.

'She doesn't stop eating!' she exclaimed, throwing her arms around me in a huge hug. 'I literally can't stop her eating,' she laughed. 'She's completely better. She has no pain and the doctor said there's no need for an operation.' Vanessa's mum had a huge smile on her face and was almost jumping with joy.

'That is fantastic news,' I cried. 'Praise God for healing her.' I looked at Ben and Joe, and they also were delighted with the news.

'Yes,' Vanessa's mum answered. 'Praise God, He healed Vanessa, and I praise God for you and your sons, for praying for my daughter. Thank you so much.'

Ben and Joe hugged me tightly, and then hugged Vanessa's mum, and we were all so overjoyed.

I am so glad I responded to that God prod. Vanessa so desperately needed a touch from God, and I am so blessed that He chose us to pray for her. Isn't that incredible – that God would choose us to be His healing hands here on this earth? What a privilege. All we need to do is be available. I know that if I hadn't responded, He would have prodded someone else, but I'm so happy He chose me.

I received another God prod while walking my dog one morning, here in São Paulo. It was a beautiful summer's day, and I was enjoying the warm weather, and the gentle early morning breeze. The sky was a brilliant shade of blue and I took a long, deep breath, grateful for this new day. I could smell the fragrance of the brightly coloured orange and pink bougainvilleas and paused to savour the moment.

I crossed the road and began to walk through the square when I caught sight of a young man sitting on a bench. He was dressed in sports clothes and had obviously just been working out at the gym or something similar. He looked like he was in his early thirties, slim and tanned, and was absorbed with something on his mobile phone.

'Go and tell him I love him,' God whispered in my ear.

'Oh, God! What if he doesn't want to know?' I replied, concerned I would be interrupting him, or make him angry.

'Go and tell him I love him,' God said gently again.

I started to walk a little slower, wondering what I should say and trying to summon up the courage to stop. Isn't that funny? I love telling people that Jesus loves them, I do it all the time and yet I still have this internal battle before I can get the words out.

This time my thoughts got the best of me, and I continued walking without stopping.

'I tell you what, God,' I said. 'If he is still here when I come back, I promise I will stop and tell him.'

Pleased with my negotiations I continued walking and almost instantly forgot all about the young man. I wandered down to the shops across the road and then about fifteen minutes later turned around to make my way home.

Arriving at the square I walked in the direction of my apartment when to my surprise I saw the young man again, who still 'happened' to be sitting on the bench.

'Oh! OK God, I get it,' I prayed. 'You really do want me to speak to this guy. I made a deal with You, and he is still here, so I will keep my word.'

Without stalling any further, I stopped in front of the bench and said, 'Hiya! Um . . . I hope you don't mind me interrupting,' I said. The young man looked up from his phone. 'But I just want to tell you that Jesus loves you.'

To my surprise the young man exclaimed, 'Oh, thank you so much,' and then to my astonishment jumped up from the bench and asked, 'Can I give you a hug?'

Now, I didn't know who was more surprised, him or me, and replied, 'Yes, of course.' He threw his arms around me and hugged me really tightly.

'What's your name?' I asked, after he returned to the bench, obviously very moved by the situation.

'Reinaldo, what's yours?' he replied.

'My name's Cally, I live in this area. How about you?'

'I've actually just moved to São Paulo,' he said. 'I'm opening a business here. I love Jesus so much and that was so amazing that you came and told me.'

'Well, to be honest,' I explained, 'He told me to tell you when I first walked past you but I didn't want to interrupt you, so I told God that if you were here on the way back then I definitely would stop – and here you are! He obviously wanted you to know!'

We chatted for several minutes, and I told him all about The Eagle Project and our work with the boys in the youth prison. He was very interested and asked me lots of questions. We swapped phone numbers and Instagram details and agreed to keep in touch.

A few weeks later I was checking the project bank account here in Brazil and his name appeared twice with two very generous donations! Isn't that amazing? God gave me a prod and the person was so touched he wanted to bless the project.

Be alert for those God prods! God so wants to use us to bless others and show them His love. When courage fails me, I go back to Mary,[15] pouring out that perfume over Jesus, risking the criticism, determined to show her love. That love that she demonstrated, that 'love that can't be contained', encourages me to step out, to be bold and allow His love to be shown.

---

15. John 12:1-8.

Questions

1. Have you felt God's prods to share your faith or bless someone?

2. Often, we talk about 'fear of man' when we think about evangelism. What does that mean to you and how can you overcome it?

3. If someone we reach out to isn't interested, how might we react in a positive way?

4. How could you support someone who is a Christian but whose husband/wife/partner isn't interested or doesn't know the Lord yet?

5. Do your neighbours, work colleagues etc. know you are a Christian? How can you be a witness to them?

6. Did you have the opportunity to show God's love to someone recently, and not carry it through? Without condemnation, reflect on this experience and ask God how you could do things differently next time.

Click on the QR code to watch the video about this chapter

Chapter Nine:

God is Taking Care of You

So do not fear, for I am with you; do not be dismayed,
for I am your God. I will strengthen you and help you;
I will uphold you with my righteous right hand.

(Isaiah 41:10)

One of the things I love about being a missionary is that deep sense of conviction that God is taking care of me in a very special way. It isn't easy to uproot and make your home in another nation, another continent and in a different culture. However, when we do it in answer to God's call, He really does take care of us.

I have so many stories to tell of God's care for me here in Brazil during the last twenty-four years. I remember sitting in a tunnel talking to some street children in the centre of São Paulo when from nowhere two policemen appeared, pointing their guns at my head. I raised my hands and wondered if I was about to meet my Maker.

The two policemen walked slowly in my direction, continuing to point their guns at me, very serious expressions on their faces. They were both in their mid to late thirties and had beer bellies spilling over the top of their trousers. When they were a few paces away from me, one of them spoke. He stared at me and frowned so hard his face reminded me of a pit bull terrier.

He spoke very slowly and deliberately in Portuguese, as if I was an alien and couldn't understand.

'We are here . . . to move the children . . . from this place,' he said. 'They come . . . down the tunnel . . . so they can steal . . . and pickpocket . . . and they can't stay here . . . Do . . . you . . . understand?'

I realised I looked like a foreigner who couldn't speak the language, so with the best Portuguese accent I could muster, I replied (speaking very quickly on purpose), 'It's OK, I understand. I'm a missionary, and I work here with the street children.'

Taken aback, both the policemen apologised and wandered off along the tunnel!

The street children all gathered round me and hugged me tightly.

'Stupid cops!' one of the boys shouted, once they were out of earshot. 'As if you would be doing anything wrong, sitting here in the tunnel talking to us.'

'Yes, Aunty,' one of the girls agreed. 'But I'm very glad they didn't shoot you.'

'Me too!' I exclaimed, and went back to explaining the activity I had brought for the children.

Another moment when I really felt God's help happened a few weeks after I arrived in São Paulo in 1999. I didn't have a car at that time so was using buses and trains to get around, and my only security was the list in my handbag of the buses and their numbers. I had to travel from my house to the *favela*, and from my house to the English school where I was giving lessons. I also needed, of course, to know how to get back home from both of those places.

My friend Adriana taught me the routes and they were the only journeys I knew how to do. If anything went wrong, I couldn't speak enough Portuguese to ask the way and would be completely lost. I didn't have a mobile phone, just a dictionary and a not very good sense of direction.

One afternoon I was travelling on a bus on the way to the English school when suddenly the heavens opened, and torrential rain began to fall. I discovered afterwards that the bus route was in an area that was prone to flooding, and within minutes the roads were impassable. The bus stopped at the side of the road and without warning, all the passengers began to get off. Not realising what was happening I sat still until everyone had left and the last passenger beckoned for me to follow.

I had no idea why everyone had got off the bus and couldn't ask what was happening. I noticed that all the passengers were walking in the same direction along the road. Several women were struggling with their small children, carrying them in their arms or dragging them along through the water.

I picked up my skirt as it was trailing in the water which was so deep in some places it was already over my knees, and began to follow the people. I put up my umbrella with some difficulty, but the rain was so heavy and it was so windy, it soon turned inside out and was a complete waste of time.

'This is crazy,' I thought. 'I am wading through knee-deep water and have no idea where I am going. Where am I going to end up? Lord, please help me!'

After walking for about five minutes, everyone turned down a side road. I felt like I was becoming more and more lost as each minute passed by. Suddenly a man who walking behind me came up to my right side, took me by the arm, and turned me around to walk back along the road in the opposite direction. We waded together through the deep water, and he led me back to the same road where the bus had stopped.

Without a word, he left me at a bus stop on the opposite side of the road to where everyone had got off the bus and then walked off.

'Thank you!' I cried as he walked away, a little startled at what had just happened.

'Who was that man? Why did he bring me here? How did he know where I am going? Now what am I going to do?' I thought.

I sat down at the bus stop, feeling like a drowned rat. The rain was running in streams down my face, and I licked my lips to quench my thirst. My feet were soaking wet, and I wiggled my toes in my new blue sandals, making a squelching sound as the water squirted out of the foam insoles.

'If that man brought me here to this bus stop, then I presume I can get a bus home from here,' I thought.

I sat and waited, peering along the road, willing a bus to come along and pick me up. What I didn't realise was that when the roads get flooded in São Paulo, it takes hours for the water level to drop and no buses would be passing by that bus stop for several hours. As I was unaware of that at the time, I sat there for two and a half hours until it began to dawn on me that maybe the bus wasn't going to come after all.

Now I realised I was really stuck. I didn't have a phone; I couldn't speak the language and it was certainly too far to walk home, even if I did know the way. One thing was for sure, I couldn't stay all night at that bus stop.

'Maybe if I try to find the English school, then I can ask Adriana to help me,' I thought. 'Lord,' I prayed. 'Please show me in which direction I need to walk.'

I stood up and started walking. The rain was still pelting the pavement and, having given up on my umbrella, I struggled along the road trying to find the shallowest puddles to wade through. My clothes weighed heavily as they clung to my sodden body and there was a strange smell in the air, like damp mixed with rotten vegetables.

I had no idea where I was going, but hoped I was walking in the right direction. The roads were eerily empty save a few other bedraggled pedestrians also trying to make their way along the rain-filled streets. I turned right down a side road off the main avenue and continued walking for a few minutes. It had been a humid and stiflingly hot day but now with the rain and my soaking wet clothes, I was beginning to feel a little cold. I shivered as I attempted to wring out my T-shirt and skirt.

'This really is crazy,' I thought to myself. I was beginning to feel quite concerned, wondering how I was going to resolve this situation. I felt quite alone and helpless and began to pray earnestly for help. 'Father, I need Your help. I am lost and I don't know what to do. Please show me the way to the English school or give me some way of finding help.'

I came to another side road and was just about to cross the street when I looked to my right and somehow it felt familiar.

'I know this road,' I thought to myself. 'I think I've been here before.' My heart began to beat faster as I walked more quickly now, hoping my instincts were right. Suddenly I found myself in front of Adriana's house, and I realised I was right, and I did know where I was! Adriana and her family ran the English school, but their house was in this road where I had miraculously found myself.

I rushed up to the front door and rang the doorbell. Adriana's brother opened the door and gasped, 'Cally, oh, my goodness, what happened? Come in quickly and get out of the rain.'

I practically fell through the front door almost crying with relief, trying to hold myself together in front of Adriana's brother. He looked down at my feet and gasped again, 'Cally, look at your feet!'

I looked down and realised the dye from my sandals had stained my feet blue!

'That is so dangerous, Cally, that rainwater is full of rats and diseases. You need to get into the shower right now. I'll get you a towel and some dry clothes.'

I was so grateful for this young man's help and willingly took a lovely hot shower, relishing the warmth of the water on my tired and stressed body. No amount of soap, however, would remove the dye from my feet, and for a month afterwards they remained a deep shade of blue. The colour gradually faded to a light turquoise and eventually returned to my normal skin colour!

Adriana arrived home shortly afterwards and was so glad that I had found my way to her house. She was very concerned when the rain began and didn't know where I was. I stayed the night and told her in quite hilarious detail about everything that had happened. We laughed a lot at my plight, but one serious question remained in my mind.

'Who was that man who appeared out of nowhere and led me to the bus stop? Why would someone do that, out of the blue, not knowing who I was or where I was going? Was it an angel?'[16]

I have a feeling it was. I just know that God took care of me that day, as always, and maybe sent an angel to rescue me. How special is that?

Have you ever been in a situation where you can almost sense the hand of God holding you? That is what I felt a few months ago when a huge lorry hit my car. It could have been a very serious car accident, even fatal, but it was another example of just how much God takes care of me. This experience was a bit of a turning point in my life, to be honest. I was by nature a rather nervous passenger, and after the accident I find myself trusting much more in God than ever before.

---

16. See Hebrews 13:2.

I was with my dear friend, Eloir, and we were travelling home from a city in Brazil called Curitiba. The publishing company, Editora Esperança, who published my first book in Portuguese are based there and we made a short visit to say 'hi' and meet the staff. All our communication up until then had been done long distance and we were anxious to meet the team in person. Eloir translated the book into Portuguese so it was very special that she could meet them too.

We stayed with our friends Jacob and Erika in their apartment, and did several wonderful days of ministry. I led a psychodrama workshop with Erika's chaplaincy team at the hospital where she works, and we led two talks for the children at a church project. I preached at the First Baptist Church at their English-speaking service, and we set aside one day for a spectacular train ride to the town of Morretes. The train travelled so high up the mountains it almost felt like we were on a plane.

Our trip ended and we travelled back to São Paulo on Sunday afternoon, very content with our few days spent in Curitiba. We could never have imagined what was about to occur.

We were driving along a notoriously dangerous motorway. It was dark, and the road was slightly wet. From nowhere, a lorry hit the side of the car and when the lorry driver swerved to avoid us, the back of his lorry pushed us into its path.

Suddenly we found ourselves being rammed along sideways, downhill, at about ninety kilometres per hour. The sound of the brakes screeching in our ears is still with me today, as the lorry driver desperately attempted to slow down. He told us afterwards that his fear was that he wasn't going to be able to stop the lorry from going over the top of us. I can't even imagine how we would have survived that or walked out of the accident without being seriously hurt.

I remember shouting 'Jesus, Jesus, Jesus' over and over again at the top of my voice, imagining at any moment that the car would flip over. Miraculously, nothing happened and the lorry came to a halt, the cabin embedded in the driver's door of the car.

People instantly came rushing to our aid. A motorist who had stopped to help opened the passenger door and asked, 'Are you all right? Are you injured?'

Eloir and I looked at each other in shock and I replied, 'No, we're fine, just a little shaken up.' We got out of the car and my legs almost buckled beneath me. I was shaking and just so grateful to be alive.

No one could believe that we were completely unharmed, and soon after an ambulance arrived which really wasn't needed. It did, however, come in handy a few minutes later.

We exchanged contact details with the lorry driver and took photos of the vehicles for the insurance claim. It was very dark on the motorway, but the lorry's headlights enabled us to see enough to share what was needed. The ambulance driver drove my car onto the hard shoulder and the lorry driver parked just a few metres in front.

We were waiting for the tow truck to arrive and standing on the hard shoulder trying to use our mobile phones. There was no signal, however, and we couldn't let anyone know what had happened.

The traffic was heavy, which was usual for a Sunday evening, with motorists and families returning home after the weekend. There was a slight build-up of traffic from curious drivers, but I felt safe next to the ambulance crew. I certainly wasn't ready for what was about to happen next.

The motorway we were travelling on isn't only notorious for serious car accidents, it is also well known for muggings and cargo theft. There have been many incidents of stones being thrown at car or lorry windscreens, causing the motorist to stop and then be mugged or even murdered. Tragically, many fatal accidents have occurred, and there are reports of the thieves having even stolen the belongings or cargo from the victims of these fatal incidents.

I knew this in the back of my mind but was so shaken up from the accident I didn't even give it a thought. I certainly didn't realise the danger we were in.

We continued waiting for the tow truck, chatting to the rescue team who were waiting for permission from the motorway police to allow the lorry driver to continue his journey. The rain had stopped, and I was still shaking, partly from the accident and partly from the chilly weather. Winter in São Paulo can be really quite cold, and the temperature can drop suddenly from a lovely warm afternoon to a cold winter's evening.

Without warning, the conversation stopped and the rescue team became tense. There were three men and one woman, all part of the ambulance crew.

One of the men turned to us and whispered, an urgent tone in his voice, 'Put your phones away, put them away, they're robbers!'

Two figures had appeared out of the bushes on the other side of the motorway. They ran swiftly across the lanes, avoiding the traffic. They were two young men, and they jumped with ease over the central reservation and sprinted in the direction of the lorry parked on the hard shoulder. To our astonishment they broke open the padlock on the back doors of the lorry, just a few metres away from us, and pulled open the doors.

The lorry driver saw what was happening and instantly raced to the cabin of the lorry and jumped in. He sped off with the back doors of the lorry flung wide open.

We hid our mobile phones in our pockets and the female paramedic called us to follow her. I didn't feel scared, even though I knew that we could be robbed. My work in prisons maybe helped me to be calm, but my dear friend Eloir was looking very worried. We raced along the hard shoulder as fast as we could, and the paramedic opened the back doors of the ambulance.

'Quickly, hide in here,' she said. 'Hopefully they won't come after you. They are more interested in the lorry and its cargo, but it's safer for you here to stay here.'

We thanked her as she left and quickly took out our phones, purses and keys and hid them in our underwear. It was one of those moments that was tragic and comical at the same time. I imagined the thieves coming into the ambulance to rob us and my belongings falling out of my underwear onto the floor!

We sat and prayed and asked God to protect us and the rescue team – they were also at the mercy of the robbers as they had no way of defending themselves. We could hardly believe the situation. Not only had we just suffered a potentially serious or fatal car accident, but we were now in danger of being robbed or even murdered.

We waited for several minutes, trying to keep calm, and eventually someone from the rescue team came to say the robbers had left. We both jumped up in relief and returned to my car to wait for the tow truck.

I can say with all honesty that I felt the hand of God on my life that night more powerfully than ever before. As I sat in that car being pushed down the hill, sideways at high speed I could literally sense that God was holding the car and stopping it from flipping over. Then when the young men arrived and left without robbing us, I saw just how closely God was once again taking care of us.

It took two and a half months for the car to be mended, and this made things very complicated for me. São Paulo is so huge and as my work with The Eagle Project takes me all over the city, a car is essential. I had to depend on taxis and public transport, but decided to make the most of new opportunities to share my faith. Every time I called an Uber, I took copies of my book with me as well as Bibles to give away, and paper and pen to write down Bible verses for the taxi drivers.

My great friend and fellow evangelist, Steve Murrill[17] always says 'look for the signs'. For example, if someone is walking with crutches, that is a sure sign that they need healing! Steve also encourages us to look for tattoos. A good conversation starter is to ask why they chose that particular tattoo and then aim to pray for them.

On one journey in the Uber, I noticed that the driver had a cross hanging from his rear-view mirror. This is quite common in Brazil, especially for Catholics who hang a cross in their car to ask God to protect them. I prayed and then said, 'I notice you have a cross hanging from your mirror. Do you mind me asking, why is that?'

The driver paused and then replied, 'That is for my brother. He was killed in a car accident, and I like to remember him every day.'

I wasn't expecting that, but it led to a conversation about heaven and earth and our relationship with God. I prayed with the driver and gave him a copy of my book before I left the car. He was so grateful and said he'd really needed to share about his brother.

I had some amazing journeys and great opportunities to bless many drivers during those two and a half months. I was able to use what could have been a frustrating time to share my faith and listen to people who needed to talk.

---

17. Steve is an evangelist at my home church, the New Life Church, Milton Keynes www. newlifechurchmiltonkeynes.org (accessed 16 January 2023); Steve teaches in the School of Supernatural Life (SSL), www.sslmk.org/ (accessed 16 January 2023).

The car accident was such a surreal experience and my whole outlook on life seemed to change after those few short moments. I have a new sense of the incredible fragility of life, of how one moment we are here and the next we are gone.

If you are considering serving God in missions, I want to encourage you to step out and trust Him. In *Dancing with Thieves*, I wrote something that I believe very firmly, that if God calls you, then you are in the centre of His will, and 'that's the safest place in the whole world'.[18]

Of course, accidents happen, and things don't always turn out how we imagine or desire, but don't allow the fear of the unknown to prevent you from stepping out. Life serving God in missions is an exciting adventure. Don't settle for the mediocre. Believe that He will take care of you, and go!

Questions

1. In what ways have you experienced God's protection in your life?

2. Do you trust God to take care of you? Why/why not?

3. Have you ever seen an angel?

4. Choose someone you know whose name begins with the same letter as yours, or the letter closest to yours, and commit to praying for them this week.

5. Accidents happen, people get injured or die. How do we reconcile our faith with these facts of life?

6. How might we come alongside people who are struggling with their faith after losing a loved one?

---

18. Magalhães, *Dancing With Thieves*, p. 186.

Click on the QR code to watch the video about this chapter

Chapter Ten:

Different Cultures and Behaviour

Don't judge of things too quickly; give yourself time to
take in the new order of things; make allowances for
what appears to you mistaken ways of doing things . . .
and where everything is not all it should be remember
that perfection is not found in this world . . .[19]

I learned many years ago that just because someone from
another culture behaves in a different way, or thinks differently,
doesn't mean it is wrong. It is just *different*! I find different
cultures fascinating, and living in Brazil for the last twenty-
four years has taught me so much about my own British
culture and that of the Brazilians.

One of their behaviour traits, for example, is a real challenge
for me. When we offer a Brazilian something to eat, they will
almost always say 'no' even if they are hungry, or they really do
want to accept. This is because their parents taught them that
it is impolite to say 'yes' straightaway. So, when they say 'no',
what they really mean is 'yes', and we need to keep insisting
until finally they admit they would like the food!

On many an occasion after guests have left my house, I have
suddenly realised I only remembered to offer them something

---

19. William Booth to his granddaughter Catherine on entering training college for The
Salvation Army in 1903. Mary Batchelor, *Catherine Bramwell-Booth* (Lion Publishing,
1986), p. 114.

once instead of insisting several times. By the time I've remembered, they are long gone!

A few years ago, a few friends from my church house group came to visit me and I carefully prepared the table for us to have some afternoon tea. As soon as everyone was ready, I took the delicious carrot and chocolate cake out of the fridge and placed it ceremoniously in the middle of the table. Everyone gasped in delight, knowing this type of cake was especially tasty.

I turned to the first friend and said, 'Would you like a piece of cake?' to which she answered shyly, 'No, thank you.'

Turning to the second friend, I asked the same question: 'And you, would you like a piece of cake?'

She also answered, smiling shyly, 'No, thank you.'

Finally, I asked the third friend, 'What about you, would you like a piece of cake?'

She answered, a little embarrassed, 'No, thank you.'

I looked at my three friends. Remembering that they were almost certainly just being polite I announced, 'So, as you know, I am British, and my *yes* is *yes*, and my *no* is *no*. I will ask you one more time and if you say no to the cake, I will happily put it away in the fridge before it melts.' In turn I asked each of my friends again, 'Would you like a piece of cake?' to which the first one answered with a giggle, 'Yes, please.'

'Would *you* like a piece of cake?' to which the second friend answered, also with a sheepish nod, 'Yes, please.'

And finally, to my third friend, ' would *you* like a piece of cake?' to which she also answered with a big smile, 'Yes, please,' and we all burst out laughing.

'That was a close one, my friends,' I said.

Having lived here for so long now, I am quite accustomed to having to insist, but something happened recently which surprised me. I went to the shopping centre to pick up my new glasses. On the first occasion I visited the opticians to choose the glasses, I made friends with Roberta, the shop assistant. She is a lovely Christian young woman and invited me to preach at her church. We have become good friends and she thoroughly enjoyed reading my first book.

I arrived in the doorway to see an elderly lady sitting at the counter and everyone in the shop singing the Brazilian version of 'Happy Birthday' (much livelier than the British version). The lady was obviously very blessed with all this special attention and my eyes were drawn to a huge piece of red velvet cake on the counter.

'Oh, Cally, how good to see you,' Roberta cried. 'Come in and sit down. Would you like a piece of cake?'

Well, of course, yes, I wanted a piece of cake. Red velvet is one of my favourite flavours and the cake looked absolutely delicious. However, a very strange thing happened. As I opened my lips, I heard myself saying, 'Oh, no, thank you,' with a polite giggle. As soon as I heard the words come out of my mouth, I was aghast and thought to myself, 'Oh no! What did I just say? Of course I want a piece of that cake. Now what am I going to do? What if she doesn't insist?'

Roberta turned to the assistant next to her and said something I couldn't hear. She turned back to me and said something else but there was a lot of noise in the shop, and I didn't catch what she said.

'Sorry, Roberta, what did you say?'

'Oh, I just told my colleague to go and get you a plate. You will have some cake, won't you?'

Not wishing to risk a second time the possibility of missing out on this amazing cake, I replied, 'Oh, of course, yes, thank you so much,' trying not to be too enthusiastic in case I appeared impolite.

The cake was indeed extremely good. A few minutes later, with my new glasses in hand, I walked out of the shop and did a little hop, skip and jump as I realised I now feel so Brazilian, I even refuse my favourite cake in an attempt to assimilate!

One of the things I really love about the Brazilians is their *joie de vivre* and their determination to make the best of sometimes very challenging situations in the hope that things will work out.

I remember visiting a place called 'Vinte Cinco de Março', near the centre of São Paulo, where there are shops that sell almost everything under the sun. That day was boiling hot, about 35 degrees Celsius or 95 degrees Fahrenheit and I stopped at a barrow serving slices of fresh pineapple and watermelon. I chose the pineapple and ate it voraciously, the juice dripping all the way down my hands to my wrists. It was absolutely delicious, so sweet and refreshing, and just what I needed.

I looked around me and saw street traders selling socks, shorts, trainers, pirated CDs, watches, pyjamas, flip flops – the list was endless. Some of the items were displayed on small tables, but most were set out on large blankets or tablecloths neatly lined up, side by side on the pavement. There was a hubbub, with the conversation of the shoppers, the shouts from the street traders and horns blaring from cars trying to make their way along the narrow streets filled with pedestrians.

I licked my lips and cleaned my sticky hands with a wet wipe and wandered into a shop to try to find some gift bags. I walked into the back of the shop and was suddenly surprised by a loud sound of people laughing wildly and shouting, coming from the street. I thought maybe it was a celebration of some kind and made my way back to the entrance of the shop to discover what was happening.

I couldn't believe my eyes as I saw a large group of street traders racing down the road, armed with their tables and blankets and wares, being chased by an army of guards.

What surprised me even more was that the street traders were laughing! It was like a huge game as they ran along the pavement, some of them dropping their wares and struggling with their tables. Others gathered up what was dropped and ran alongside to return the goods to their owners.

I was impressed at how they had obviously folded up their blankets or tables at high speed with their products tucked inside, in order to be able to run away at a moment's notice.

The guards were shouting for them to stop and were huffing and puffing as they tried to catch up. Some were middle-aged men with big beer bellies and obviously not fit enough to run very fast. It was like a comedy film but also so sad as I realised that these street traders were just trying to make a living. Most of this trading is illegal, as they require a permit and at any moment the street traders are forced to flee from the council 'police' who arrive without warning and seize their merchandise.

That day it struck me how Brazilians are so resilient and have such a positive attitude. No one was swearing or retaliating, they were just trying to escape without losing their wares. Almost everyone escaped without incident, but I saw some of the traders walking back down the street, empty-handed and with very sad expressions on their faces. Most of these few were elderly and had obviously not got away in time.

'I suppose now they will need to use any money they have to buy new stock instead of food for their families,' I thought.

I turned to go back into the shop when out of the corner of my eye I saw an old lady, walking slowly along the pavement, her head hung low, her shoulders hunched over. She was dressed in an old pair of tracksuit bottoms and a faded blouse. As she passed me, she looked up, and I saw that she was crying.

'Did you lose your things?' I asked.

'Yes,' she replied, sobbing. 'I just started selling here yesterday and now I will have to start all over again. I was just trying to help my son and his wife. He just lost his job, and they can't pay their rent.'

'I'm so sorry,' I replied, feeling sad for this elderly lady, struggling so hard to earn some money, and obviously devastated by the situation. 'I'm afraid I can't pay for you to buy your goods again, but could I pray for you and ask God to bless you and your family?' I asked gently.

'Oh, yes, please,' she replied. 'I believe God is with me.'

I placed my hand on her shoulder and prayed a simple prayer, asking for God's blessing and provision for this dear lady.

'Amen!' she cried at the end of the prayer, and threw her arms around me. 'Thank you, thank you so much,' she said. 'I will keep trusting in God to help me and my family. Sometimes He is all I have.'

I took a note out of my purse and placed it in her hand. It wasn't very much money, but she hugged me again and cried, 'God bless you, my dear, God bless you for praying for me. Thank you so much.'

She went on her way, continuing to walk slowly, but with her head held high now, obviously hopeful for a new start. I turned to go back into the shop and continued with my errands for that day, praying for the lady and her family, grateful to have been able to pray for her.

This book began with the story of Mary pouring out the perfume, and Jesus' reaction to her act of sacrifice and love:

'Leave her alone,' Jesus replied. 'It was intended that she should save this perfume for the day of my burial. You will always have the poor among you, but you will not always have me.'

(John 12:7-8)

Jesus stated a truth. The poor will always be among us. That is a tragic fact, but when we are faced with situations like this, if we can't change the situation financially, we can always offer to pray or show God's love in some way.

Finally, here, I would like to share with you one of my most embarrassing problems with the Brazilian language. I enjoy most foods but really don't like coconut and always used to ask if there was any in cakes or biscuits that I was served. This, however, made my life very complicated, especially in the first few years that I lived in Brazil, when I was still learning to speak Portuguese and pronounce the words correctly.

The Portuguese word for coconut is 'coco' with the stress on the first syllable, 'co'. Unfortunately for me, however, the Portuguese word for '*poo*' is cocô, with the stress on the second syllable, 'cô'. Soon after arriving in Brazil the first time, I asked if a cake had any coconut in it, but I actually asked if there was any 'poo' in the cake!

My host was taken aback and laughed loudly at my mistake. I, of course, had no idea what was going on as I couldn't hear or pronounce the difference between these two words at all. It was all in good humour of course, no one was being unkind, but the Brazilians did find it extremely funny.

The problem was that it took me ages to get it right. I was always very careful to practise the pronunciation several times before opening my mouth. I would find a quiet corner to rehearse saying, 'Does this cake have coconut in it? 'Does this cake have coconut in it? 'Does this cake have coconut in it?' After a few moments, when I felt confident enough that I had perfected the intonation, I would go and ask the host, 'Does this cake have poo in it?'

I resolved this problem by just eating any cake I was served and hoping it wasn't made with coconut! I am now able to hear the difference between the two sounds and strangely enough, don't even need to ask any more as I quite enjoy coconut these days!

Learning to live in a different culture is certainly a challenge and these are just a few of my experiences and mistakes. On reflection, I think my own struggles and errors have made me more gracious towards people of other cultures. It is so essential that we try to understand others and not think that we're the ones who are right and everyone else is wrong. I truly love Brazil and the Brazilian culture, and feel very grateful and privileged that God called me here to serve this beautiful nation and its people.

Questions

1. What are some of the different culture traits of those around you, in your workplace, neighbourhood etc?

2. What in your opinion is one of the best traits of your culture?

3. What in your opinion is one of the least favourable traits of your culture?

4. How can you adapt your culture traits so you can be more like Jesus to the people around you?

5. It is usual that people of other cultures have different religions. Have you tried to share your faith with people of other religions? How did that work out?

6. Pray that God will give you opportunities to show His love to members of other people groups or religions.

Click on the QR code to watch the video about this chapter

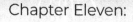

Chapter Eleven:

Just Being There

The Spirit of the Sovereign Lord is on me,
because the Lord has anointed me
to proclaim good news to the poor.
He has sent me to bind up the broken-hearted,
to proclaim freedom for the captives
and release from darkness for the prisoners…

(Isaiah 61:1)

An aspect of the Brazilian culture which is so desperately sad and unjust is the extreme poverty. When I began working with the street kids in the year 2000 I often found myself in places that were so incredibly poor it was almost impossible to bear.

One day in the year 2001 I went to visit a young couple who I had met on the streets. I arrived in their road and realised their home was through a hole in the wall.

'Can it really be possible they live here?' I thought. 'Surely, they don't live in this place with their babies as well?'

A sick feeling welled up in my stomach as I realised this was the right address. I had become acquainted with Paulo and Marcia and their friends Antonio and Tania after meeting them on a few occasions. The last time we met they had invited me to their 'home', and this was my first visit.

I lowered my head to go through the hole and began to pick my way in the darkness through the debris to the corner of the building. I had brought some nappies and some basic foods, and I remembered Marcia's instructions: 'When you go in, Aunty, go to the far left corner and that is our home.' I could indeed make out a small room in the darkness and could see a faint light coming from under the door.

Even though I could see the room I wasn't sure how I was going to get there. Before me was what seemed like an assault course of various wooden crates and old furniture strewn across the space. The floor was ankle-deep in filthy sewage water and I carefully tottered across some planks that had been precariously placed where the water was deeper.

The air was thick with the stench of urine, and I hoped and prayed I wouldn't slip and fall. The planks were unstable and several times I nearly lost my balance, but just manged to keep from falling into the 'water' below me.

My thoughts kept returning to the babies who belonged to these two couples. I had met them several times with their children, so I knew they often carried them out of here to go to the streets.

'It's so dangerous,' I thought. 'When they cross these planks with the babies in their arms, oh, my Lord, it's unthinkable what would happen if they fell into this water. I know they use drugs and are often drunk, so the possibility of an accident is so high. Oh, Lord, please help them find somewhere better to live.'

My thoughts were interrupted by the sight of Antonio, who had appeared in the doorway of their room. He was in his early twenties, short and stocky with long, curly dark hair. His arms and legs were covered in mosquito bites and his lips were full of sores.

'Aunty, you're here!' he exclaimed. 'We were waiting for you. Come in. Welcome to our home.'

Their 'home' was a small, damp room with two filthy mattresses on the floor, a rusty old cooker and an even rustier fridge. Clothes were piled up around the edges of the room, left up against the walls, thick with black mould. The air was stiflingly hot as it was the height of summer and as always, I felt the sweat beginning to drip down my back.

Marcia and Tania were both sitting on the mattresses, their babies propped up on their laps, bottles of milk hanging out of their mouths. Marcia was slender and pale-skinned, with long, dark hair and sunken eyes. She didn't look well, and I wondered if maybe she was anaemic.

Tania was taller than Marcia and extremely skinny. Her hair was scraped back into a low ponytail, and it looked like she hadn't washed it for days. Looking around me I realised there was no bathroom, and it was obvious they wouldn't be able to shower or bathe easily – the adults or their babies.

I sat down next to Marcia on the mattress, after bending down to hug them both. Marcia's baby, Mariana, was just six months old, with jet-black curly hair and pale skin. She was very tiny and thin and obviously having difficulty breathing. A loud rasping sound came from her chest every time she tried to breathe in to take another gulp of milk.

'I think she might have pneumonia, Aunty,' Marcia explained. 'It's so damp in here and she's just had a bad cold. Last night she suddenly got worse and has been like this ever since.'

Mariana spat the teat of the bottle out and coughed a deep, rattly cough before her mother thrust the bottle back into her mouth.

'It sounds like you might be right, Marcia,' I replied. 'She sounds very congested. Did you take her to the doctor?'

'Yes, I took her yesterday. He said to go back today to do inhalation. I'm just waiting for Paulo to get home. He shouldn't be long, and then we'll take her.'

'I wonder what Paulo is up to,' I thought. 'Maybe he went out to steal, or to get drugs?' He certainly wasn't at work, that was for sure.

'How about Junior, Tania? Is he OK?' I asked. Junior was Tania's three-month-old son, dark-skinned and with a mop of brown, curly hair covering his forehead. He was also undernourished and extremely small for his age.

'He's fine, Aunty,' she replied, her voice faint with tiredness. She yawned and continued, 'He wasn't sleeping well at night, so now I'm adding cornflour to his bottle and that seems to be working.'

'Cornflour?' I asked, astonished she was giving him that at such a young age. 'Why cornflour?'

'That's what my mum always gave me, and my brothers and sisters, and it seems to do the trick,' she replied. 'It thickens the milk and keeps him asleep until the morning.'

'Try to only use it if you *really* need to,' I suggested gently. 'Babies' insides are very sensitive and just milk would be better at this age.'

'Aw, Aunty, I need my beauty sleep,' she laughed, and I had a feeling she wouldn't take my advice. I was sad that both the babies were drinking formula milk instead of being breastfed. Unfortunately, many of the street girls don't persist with breastfeeding and give up very quickly, or don't even try at all. This, of course, means they must buy formula milk, which is expensive and obviously not as healthy as breast milk.

'We bought some fizzy drink for your visit,' Marcia said, getting up from the mattress with some difficulty. 'And Tania made a cake!'

'Oh, you're so kind,' I exclaimed. 'You really didn't need to go to all this trouble just for me.'

'You're not trouble, Aunty,' Marcia replied. 'We never have any visitors here, so we wanted to celebrate your visit.'

I was moved by their thoughtfulness. I could tell they were so pleased I had made the effort to visit them, and helped them pour out the fizzy drink into plastic cups. Tania served me a slice of cake on a piece of paper towel, and I ate it politely, trying not to imagine the extreme lack of sanitation involved in its preparation. It would be so rude to refuse it after she had made it just for my visit, so I prayed and asked God to bless my stomach.

I felt so sad to see these two families literally holed up in this awful place, and wondered if they would ever make it to live in a better home. Marcia was holding Mariana in the crook of her arm and suddenly the baby began to squawk loudly. Marcia looked down and saw the child's dummy had fallen on the dirt floor. She quickly bent down, licked it and stuffed it back in Mariana's mouth.

My thoughts went back to my own home and my sometimes over-paranoid care with Benjamin, my baby son, who was just a few months old at the time. Images of bottle sterilisers and wiping and washing of toys flashed through my mind.

'I think I might be a bit more relaxed after this,' I thought, reflecting on Benjamin's immune system. 'If these two can survive this, I am sure I don't need to be so worried about Ben. But this must be one of the worst places I have ever visited. They need to find somewhere better to live, somewhere less damp and with some windows and natural light.'

My mind began to wander, imagining the dangers of the babies learning to crawl and walk in that place. Mariana began to cough, a deep chesty cough that left her breathless and limp. I didn't like the sound of it at all and laid the back of my hand gently on her neck. She was boiling hot and obviously had a high temperature.

Paulo appeared in the doorway at that moment; I was relieved that he had arrived at last. However, he seemed to be drunk or high on drugs and was swaying from side to side. He was tall and surly looking, with short, dark hair hidden under his cap.

A few minutes later, we were all crossing the planks and leaving the building. I gave Paulo, Marcia and Mariana a ride to the hospital while Antonio and Tania headed off to the streets with Junior.

About ten minutes later, we arrived at the entrance to the emergency room.

'Would you like me to wait with you?' I asked Marcia.

'Oh, no, Aunty, we'll probably be here for hours. The queue is always so long. Please just go home and we'll let you know how she is later today. Thank you so much for coming to visit us, it meant such a lot to us that you came.'

I prayed with the three of them and waved goodbye. My heart was so heavy with the reality of these young people's lives. All of them had lived on the streets since they were children, and I felt so lost as to how to help or know what difference I could make.

The reality was that I could do very little except pray. I could take them food parcels and nappies but that wouldn't change their situation. I felt like I was trying to dress a deep, open wound with a very small plaster.

A few weeks later, I discovered that Antonio and Paulo had both been arrested for stealing cars and put in prison. In a funny kind of way, it was an answer to prayer, as it made the girls move out of that terrible place. Marcia moved into a Catholic home for young mothers and did very well for many years, raising Mariana and another daughter she had along the way.

Tania also found somewhere else to live and brought up Junior by herself, along with the other children she gave birth to as a result of prison visits with Antonio. Yes, incredible as it is, many infants are born in Brazil every year whose fathers are in prison –the babies are conceived through 'intimate visits'. Despite counselling on birth control and the use of condoms, the macho Brazilian culture sadly lends itself to this reality of men in prison fathering children, and being absent from their families.

Sometimes it is impossible to change situations. However, so often it is possible to make a difference. A few weeks ago, a boy who we worked with in the youth prison was sent home and my team went to visit him and his family. They arrived to find a terrible situation where the whole family was sleeping on the floor, literally, with no beds or mattresses. This kind of situation can often lead a boy from the youth prison to reoffend simply to be sent back to prison, where at least he has a bed and food.

We bought a triple bunk bed for the family and paid for a van to help them move to a better home. The boy and his family were so grateful, and we were relieved to have been able to help. We were delighted to hear that they are now fine, the boy is working and something as simple as a bunk bed made such a huge difference.

One of my favourite sayings is the quote we have stamped on the back of our Eagle Project T-shirts:

It is impossible for one person to change the world. But it is possible to change the world for one person.[20]

I can't make a huge difference most of the time, but every day I can try to make a small difference. And you can too!

---

20. Anonymous.

Questions

1. How can we treat the poor with dignity?

2. When you see someone who is begging, do you give them money? If yes, why? If no, why not?

3. Are there people known to you that are in seemingly impossible situations? Think about them now.

4. Have you tried to help someone in a difficult situation and found new ways to help that you didn't imagine were possible?

5. If we can't help financially or practically, what else can we do to help people who are suffering, or what else can we give?

6. Are there circumstances in your own life that you know you can't practically change? Is there anyone you trust enough to share your problems, and ask them to pray, believing God has the power to change people and situations?

Click on the QR code to watch the video about this chapter

Chapter Twelve:

Take Risks for Jesus!

Our prayers may be awkward. Our attempts may
be feeble. But since the power of prayer is in the
One who hears it and not in the one who says it,
our prayers do make a difference.[21]

It isn't easy stepping out of our comfort zone to share our faith. Maybe you feel like sometimes you step out alone and just hope God shows up. I think often I have felt like that, but have many stories that prove He really does show up and that has increased my faith even more.

In Acts 1:8, Jesus told His disciples they would receive power when the Holy Spirit came upon them and I believe that this same power is available for us. The truth is that the Holy Spirit is always with us, He dwells in us as 1 Corinthians 3:16 tells us, and we should draw on His anointing power every time we step out for the Lord. I believe our heavenly Father loves it when we take risks for Him, and I hope these stories encourage you to step out with boldness and faith.

A few years ago, I studied for a postgraduate in psychodrama here in São Paulo and made some lovely friends during the two years of study. They all knew I was a Christian and I always looked for opportunities to bless them and pray with them.

---

21. Max Lucado, *Max on Life: Discovering the Power of Prayer* (New York: HarperCollins, 2007).

One evening I left the college with my friend at the end of our lecture, and we walked in the direction of her car.

'See you next week, then,' I said. 'Take care, and safe journey home.'

'Thanks, Cally,' she replied. 'Safe journey too.'

I paused just to make sure she had got into her car safely when I saw her fumbling in her rucksack, obviously looking for something.

'Cally, I can't find my keys,' she exclaimed, a hint of panic in her voice. It was late at night and São Paulo is not a safe place to hang around in the street after dark. 'I always put them in my rucksack, but I can't find them anywhere! Maybe they dropped on the ground when I parked?'

She was looking in each pocket and inside the rucksack too. We began to scour the ground around and beneath the car, hoping the keys would be there. We used the torches on our mobile phones to make the task a little easier, but the keys were nowhere to be found.

A thought came into my mind that I should offer to pray and ask God to help us.

'I have an idea,' I said. 'I'm going to pray and ask God to help us find your keys. After all, He knows where they are, even if we don't. I always do that when I lose something, and He has helped me on so many occasions.' I prayed a short, simple prayer out loud, nothing super-spiritual. 'Father, we need to find the car keys. Please could You help us? Please show us where they are. Amen!'

'I hope that works,' my friend replied, not very convincingly. I knew she wasn't a Christian and I so wanted her to see the miracle happening. We continued looking and after a few minutes I began to have a serious chat with God.

'Father, I really need You to answer that prayer. I have stepped out and put my faith on the line. Please could You show me where the keys are? I so want my friend to know You and realise that You care for even the small details of our lives.'

My friend had gone back to looking around the car and I felt I should look in a certain pocket in her rucksack.

'I have a feeling they are here,' I announced.

'I have already looked there, Cally,' my friend said. 'I have searched every pocket of that rucksack.'

'But I feel like they are here,' I replied, and stuck my hand deep down into an inside pocket.

'Come on, God, You can do this,' I prayed, and heard a jingle at the end of my fingertips. I grabbed the bunch of keys at the very bottom of the pocket and held them up triumphantly for my friend to see.

'Are these the ones?' I asked.

'Cally!' my friend shrieked, running over to my side. 'I am going to start going to your church!' She hugged me really tightly, and we both jumped up and down in excitement.

I drove home, praising and worshipping God for hearing my prayer and showing my friend that He is real and answers when we pray.

I took a risk that night. But what if I'd prayed and we didn't find the keys? That is a very real possibility; however, I have discovered that the more I step out for God, believing He will answer, the more He delights in showing up.

I have another wonderful story to share with you, but this time it was me who was on the receiving end of the prayer. It was 1986 and I was in my final year studying at Nonington College, for a BA Honours degree from the University of Kent at Canterbury.

A group of us were rehearsing for a show called 'Stepping Out', about a tap dance class, and I had the main role as the tap dance teacher. The script was memorised, the dance routines were polished, and the following Monday was opening night.

The Saturday before the show was the long-awaited Summer Ball, a lively party held on the lawn, complete with steel band and cocktails. It was a beautiful summer's day, with a gentle wind, and the students and staff were chatting and laughing together. The cocktails were delicious and tasted more like strawberry lemonade than anything alcoholic. I drank rather too many, unfortunately, and while dancing rather boisterously to the sound of the steel band lost my balance and fell to the ground. As I fell, my ankle twisted badly and I cried out in terrible pain.

My first thought was: 'Oh no! The show! Now what am I going to do?'

The director of the show, who also happened to be my drama teacher, was one of the first to help me to my feet. He was a kind, gentle man and I could tell he was very concerned. I stood on my good leg and winced in pain as I looked down at my ankle, already swelling to the size of a tennis ball.

'I'm sorry,' I whined, looking at the expression of dismay on my drama teacher's face.

'Do you think it's broken, Cally?' he asked hesitantly, staring aghast at my ankle. I could tell exactly what he was thinking. I didn't have an understudy and if I couldn't dance, then the show was over before it had even begun.

'I don't know,' I replied, trying to hold back the tears. 'I really hope not.'

One of my friends, the only person sober on the campus, drove me to hospital, and I sat in the casualty department feeling very despondent.

'I can't believe this has happened,' I thought. 'One minute I was dancing and the next I wasn't. How am I going to get better in two days?'

A few hours later and the results of the X-ray revealed a bad sprain.

'You're lucky it isn't broken,' the doctor said. 'That's what you get for dancing in high heels! My advice is lots of ice and rest it as much as possible. If you can keep your foot up for the next few days that will help the swelling.'

'Actually,' I replied, and took a deep breath, trying to choose my words carefully, 'I am supposed to be performing in a play on Monday. I have the main part and I'm the tap dance teacher. I'll be fine to do it, won't I?' I asked hopefully.

The young doctor looked at me over the rim of his glasses. He paused and shook his head. I realised it was not going to be good news.

'I am sorry, young lady, no dancing for you for at least a few weeks. You have a nasty sprain and if you put weight on your foot too soon, you could do yourself some serious damage.'

'Really?' My eyes welled up with tears. I didn't want to cry there in the hospital, but I was so disappointed and worried about what my drama teacher and my classmates would think. I was letting everyone down and we had rehearsed so hard for so many weeks.

The doctor saw my expression and patted the back of my hand. 'I'm sorry. Get yourself back to college now. And,' he paused and winked cheekily, 'no more boogying to the steel band!'

I forced a giggle, and my friend wheeled me out of the room and took me to her car.

The next day was Sunday, and my ankle was still very swollen and sore. I sent a message to my drama teacher saying I would try to do the show, but I knew the reality was I could hardly walk, let alone dance. I was sitting forlornly in my room with a friend, my foot up on a chair and a sick feeling in my stomach.

Scenes from the show kept flashing through my mind.

'Maybe that scene I wouldn't have to dance,' I reasoned with myself, 'and in that other scene maybe we could add in a line asking one of my students to try to teach the routine? Perhaps I could do the show sitting in a wheelchair?' The whole show raced through my mind as I tried to find a solution for each scene in which I had to dance and other possibilities for the choreography.

In the end, I realised it was pointless. I couldn't do the show sitting down. I put my head in my hands as the reality set in.

Knock, knock.

'Is that someone at my door?' I asked.

'Who can that be?' my friend said.

'Come in!' I called.

Two people, a young man and a young woman, popped their heads around the door.

'We're so sorry to interrupt,' the young woman said, 'but we were at the Summer Ball yesterday. We're former Nonington students, and we saw you fall and hurt your ankle.'

'Oh, hi,' I replied. 'Yeah, it's badly sprained.'

She paused and then said, 'Is it OK if we come in?'

Slightly confused and wondering why these people were there, I answered, 'Yes, um . . . come in.'

The young couple walked into the room. They both looked in their mid-twenties, the young man was tall and dark-haired and the young woman, medium height and blonde. They were both smiling, a little shyly, and the young man said, 'Um . . . so . . . we're Christians, and we believe in healing, and we wondered if we could pray for you? For God to heal your ankle?' The young woman nodded in agreement.

There was an awkward silence.

My first thought was to just crack up laughing, but I managed to control myself. I looked at my friend and could tell she was also trying not to laugh. I knew some of the students from the Christian Union at the college and to be honest, I thought they were a bunch of weirdos. Baptisms in the swimming pool, campus prayer walks, singing worship songs while strumming guitars and super-spiritual behaviour – I wasn't impressed at all.

My next thought was to just get rid of them and say I didn't want them to pray for me. However, something stopped me sending them away.

'What if God does heal me and I'm able to do the play? What do I have to lose?' I thought.

The couple were standing in front of me, patiently waiting for my response. They seemed so friendly and kind.

'Yeah, OK,' I replied, nonchalantly. I didn't want them to think I believed in all this healing stuff, but at the same time I desperately needed a miracle.

The couple knelt down beside my leg and placed their hands on my ankle. It all felt a bit weird as I certainly wasn't used to this kind of thing, but I shut my eyes and tried to concentrate as they began to pray.

'Lord, we are here to ask You for a miracle.' The young man prayed quietly but loud enough for us to hear. 'Our friend needs your healing. Please heal her ankle, take away all the pain and swelling, and help her to be well. In Jesus' name we pray. Amen.'

We all opened our eyes and the young woman said, 'Try to walk on it to see if it's better.'

I lifted myself up out of my chair and steadied myself on the desk beside me.

'This is crazy,' I thought. 'As if God is going to heal me here in my room!'

I carefully placed my foot on the floor, and strangely enough, it seemed to feel a little better. I could put my weight on it without feeling a stabbing pain through my ankle.

'Mmm,' I said. 'It feels a little better.'

'That's great,' the young man cried. 'God is healing you! Let's pray again for complete healing!' And he fell to his knees and prayed once more, 'Thank You, Lord, thank You for Your healing power, now please complete the healing!' He jumped to his feet enthusiastically and asked, 'How does it feel now?'

It felt just the same.

'Thank you for praying. I'm sure I will be fine,' I said. I really didn't believe that God was going to heal me and said that just to get rid of them.

'Yes, you will be fine,' the young man replied. 'God is already healing you. Well, sorry again for the interruption, goodbye, and take care.'

They scurried out of the door, seemingly as anxious to leave as I was for them to be gone.

My friend and I waited a few seconds, looked at each other and burst out laughing. We almost cried, laughing for several minutes, and I tried to speak.

'Can you believe that? As if God would heal me!' I said in disbelief.

Several minutes later we managed to compose ourselves but promised each other we would never forget that hilarious moment.

The next day I woke up early in the morning. It was Monday and the day of the show. I swung my legs carefully out of the bed preparing to hop to the bathroom and when I looked down at my ankle, it was less swollen than the day before. I carefully placed my foot on the floor and was able to walk! I did a few slow paces and realised my ankle was feeling much better.

'Let me try a few tap dance steps,' I thought, and gingerly tried a few shuffle ball changes. A few moments later I came to the amazing conclusion that I wasn't in pain and that I would be able to dance that evening. I didn't make any connection with the prayer from the day before, and certainly didn't give God the credit for healing me. I just thought my ankle had somehow got better by itself.

That evening I took part in the show and was able to do all the dance routines. I danced the following night, too, and the show was a great success. It was only many years later, when I became a Christian, that I realised what had happened that day. God had healed my ankle and did a miracle in my life. I didn't acknowledge Him, or thank Him, but He healed me anyway.

I will always remember that couple and the great courage they showed that day. I still try to imagine them talking about my accident and making the brave decision to go to my room and offer to pray for me.

They were so sweet and kind and although I wasn't rude, I certainly wasn't very gracious in my attitude towards them. Their act of faith made an impact on my life even though I didn't realise it at the time. The courage they showed still inspires me to this day and encourages me to step out and take risks for God.

I don't know their names, so have never been able to find them, but I would love to be able to thank them and tell them my story. Their act of faith made a director very relieved, a drama class very happy and gave a missionary in Brazil a great story to tell.

I hope this story encourages you to step out and take risks for God. People may laugh, reject you or insult you, but every act of faith is a seed sown in someone's life. You are extending the kingdom of God every time you step out and make Him known. Keep going, step out of your comfort zone and keep taking risks.

I also want to encourage you to always aim to pray. When we speak to someone or help them, that is important and shows

God's love. But when we *pray*, that is when we move from the natural to the supernatural. That is when God's power is shown, and heaven comes to earth.

Many years ago, I visited a family in one of the poorest *favelas* in São Paulo. There was no basic sanitation, the floor of the rickety wooden shack was just dirt and dust, and the family told me that rats ran over them at night. Just as I arrived, I saw a huge rat run from beneath the shack and into the dwelling next door. I don't like rats at all and hoped it wasn't intending to return.

The hot summer air was filled with the stench of rotting food, discarded nappies and sewage water. I clapped my hands outside the shack, the Brazilian equivalent of ringing the doorbell, and several children popped their heads around the door.

'Hi, Aunty, come in! Mummy's just feeding the baby,' the eldest announced.

The mother had recently given birth to her sixth child and was seated on a torn and broken sofa with the baby at her breast. She was in her thirties but looked at least fifty years old. Her hair was long and matted and she was extremely thin and frail. I wondered how the baby would develop, as she was certainly using drugs and drinking alcohol during the pregnancy.

'She dropped out on the floor here in the doorway before I could even get to the hospital,' she exclaimed. I looked at the filthy, dusty floor and shuddered at the thought of this tiny little baby beginning its life there among the dirt. 'My neighbour came and cut the umbilical cord. I s'pose when you get to the sixth, they just drop out without warning,' she joked.

I tried not to imagine the scene and was concerned for this family, a new baby arriving one after the other into such poverty and squalor. Both the parents were drug users, and the children were all filthy and malnourished. (Eventually the social services took all the children into care for a while but somehow the parents managed to persuade the judge to give them back.)

I arrived that day with food parcels and nappies, and several of the children climbed onto my lap as we chatted. When it was time to leave, I offered to pray.

'Let me just call my neighbour and her children,' the mother exclaimed. 'They will want you to pray for them too.'

A few moments later, a young woman arrived with her two small children and teenage daughter.

'I heard you were here,' the woman said gently. 'We would love you to pray for us too.'

'Of course,' I replied, and we all stood in a circle and held hands, the two families squashed into the tiny shack, hot as a sauna.

I was halfway through the prayer when the teenage girl began to exclaim, 'Oh, I can feel God! I can feel Him, I feel like there's electricity running through me. My whole body is tingling!'

I had shut my eyes to pray, and on reflection, it is best to bow your head but always keep your eyes open! I looked up and saw that the girl had a huge smile on her face and was shaking her hands and arms.

'I can feel Jesus!' she cried, and it was obvious that she was experiencing the power of God in a very real way. We all began to pray again and thank God and laugh and jump up and down.

It was such an amazing moment that I have never forgotten, and one that encourages me always to aim to pray. When we pray, that is when God breaks in and brings freedom and healing. When we pray, He shows His power and people's lives are transformed.

Aim to pray. And don't be surprised when God shows up!

Questions

1. Have you ever taken a risk and prayed for someone you don't know? What happened?

2. Has anyone ever prayed for you that didn't know you and was obviously stepping out and taking a risk in order to bless you?

3. What signs can we look for to know that someone needs prayer?

4. What ways might God speak to you to step out and take a risk?

5. It is better to step out in faith and get it wrong than to not step out at all?

6. Pray for opportunities to step out and take risks for God.

Click on the QR code to watch the video about this chapter

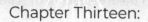

Chapter Thirteen:

Be Expectant

Ask and it will be given to you; seek and you will find;
knock and the door will be opened to you. For everyone
who asks receives; the one who seeks finds; and to the
one who knocks, the door will be opened.

(Matthew 7:7-8)

Have you ever felt a call to step out and serve God in long-term missions? If you didn't respond to that call, then please think carefully for a few moments. What was it that stopped you?

For many people, the answer is a lack of funds or an uncertainty that God will provide. Living by faith is not easy, but it certainly is exciting! Money doesn't fall out of the sky, so when we serve God as missionaries that money must come from somewhere. I have so many wonderful stories of God's provision and His very creative ways of blessing me.

Years ago, my husband (at the time) and I decided to try to buy a house in a little town 50 kilometres outside São Paulo. It was George's desire to move away from the city, and the properties were so much cheaper further away. We sold my house in Milton Keynes for £40,000, and one of the first things we did was discuss how we should give the tithe.[22] We felt we

---

22. See for example Malachi 3:8-10 about the principle of giving a tithe, that is, 10 per cent, to the Lord's work.

should divide it between our church in Milton Keynes and our church in São Paulo.

As soon as the money was transferred to my bank account, we sent a message to the treasurer of the church, my dear friend Roger Clarke, to let him know that a cheque for £2,000 would be on its way to the church bank account. Roger is a pastor and a faithful man of God and someone who demonstrates a real love for the Lord. He phoned later that day and said, 'Hi, Cally, I'm just phoning about the cheque you sent. Thank you so much but you're missionaries. You do realise you don't need to give that tithe?'

'Hi, there,' I answered. 'I understand, but we want to give it, Roger. We prayed about how to give the tithe, and this is what we want to do.'

'But Cally,' Roger replied, 'you know people don't normally tithe money from house sales as the money's just transferred to the bank for the next mortgage payments. Honestly, Cally, thank you so much, but you really don't need to give this money.'

'But we *want* to, Roger,' I replied with even more enthusiasm. 'Please accept the money and use it as God leads you.'

There was a pause and then Roger said with great emotion in his voice, 'Well, Cally, if I can't persuade you otherwise, then thank you so much. God bless you both for your hearts to give.'

'Thanks, Roger, God bless you too,' I replied. 'We'll see you at church on Sunday.'

Later that day Roger phoned me with some wonderful news.

'Cally, I just wanted to let you know that the tithe you gave is going to help the people in Mostar, in Bosnia. I was literally crying out to God yesterday for money to pay for the lorry to take all the supplies we have received. The offering you gave is exactly the amount we need to be able to send the lorry. I thought you and George would like to know!'

My heart was full of joy, and I replied, 'Thank you so much for letting me know, Roger, that's wonderful news. It's even more special for me because I remember my time in Mostar with such fondness. What a blessing!'

A few days later, we travelled back to São Paulo, and soon afterwards exchanged the rest of the tithe into Brazilian reais. The exchange rate at the time was three Reais to the sterling pound so we had 6,000 reais to give as a tithe to our church.

It felt a bit crazy in a way. We had so little spare cash and I was concerned about how we would buy everything we needed for Benjamin, who was soon to be born. I imagined putting him to bed in a cardboard box as we certainly had no money to buy a cot.

We went to church the following Sunday evening and in my handbag was an envelope stuffed with 6,000 reais. When it was time for the offering, I went to the front of the church to put the envelope in the box. It was such an incredible feeling. I was in a large church with hundreds of people around me, but it felt like this moment was just me and God. I had the most overwhelming sense of joy bubbling up inside me, and a desire to dance in delight. I returned to my seat and sat and cried for a few minutes, so grateful for God's provision in our lives.

A few weeks later, we found a house that we wanted to buy. It was a big property and would be perfect for our family and to receive visitors and teams from the UK. The only problem was that the owner had set the asking price at 250,000 reais and we had just 114,000. We didn't know how we would be able to pay for it, but we prayed and asked God to do a miracle.

A few days later our friend who helped us with our finances in the UK called and said, 'Hi, Cally, I just phoned to let you know I have some amazing news. You have received an anonymous offering of £8,000! I am just transferring it to your account.'

'What? That is such fantastic news. Oh, my goodness,' I cried, jumping up and down! I began to do the maths in my head and realised that after exchanging £8,000 into reais we now had £130,000 reais, still a long way off but getting closer to our goal.

The owner of the house lived a long way from São Paulo, but arranged to meet us at the house to talk. He was a lovely Christian man who was very well off and spent much of his money helping to build churches. He and his wife received us with a warm welcome and they took us into the lounge to sit down. I was now about five months' pregnant with Benjamin and beginning to feel tired most of the time. I sat and wondered how this was going to go. I knew the owner was asking for a much higher price than the money we had available, and I tried to keep my faith high for a miracle.

After a few minutes of introductions and chit chat, the owner of the house said gently, 'Well, let me tell you what has happened. I set the price of the house at 250,000 reais, but it hasn't sold. In fact, the house has been on the market for eleven years and even though several people have shown interest, I have never felt it was the right moment to sell.' He paused. 'A few weeks ago, I had a dream. I dreamed that a young couple in ministry would come to me and ask to buy the house, and I felt God tell me to lower the price.' He paused and smiled.

My heart began to beat faster, and I looked at George and raised my eyebrows.

'Could that young couple be us?' I thought. 'I wonder what price he will ask?'

The owner continued. He was obviously feeling very emotional, and his voice was shaking slightly as he spoke. 'So, I felt this was God speaking to me. I have prayed about this with my wife.' I looked at her and she nodded. 'And we have decided to lower the price to ...'

I felt like my heart was going to stop beating and I held my breath waiting for what he was going to say.

'To ... 130,000 reais.'

I gasped. George nodded at me, and his face broke into a huge smile. We both knew that was exactly the amount of money we had in the bank.

Then suddenly I remembered Benjamin and the cot and all the other things we needed to buy. My heart sank as I realised the price of the house was going to use up all our money and we would have absolutely nothing to spare. The house was large, and we would need to buy kitchen furniture and wardrobes and beds. I wanted to be happy, but we had so many needs beyond just the purchase of the house.

The owner's voice broke into my thoughts.

'And we have decided we will sell the house "doors shut".'

'Doors shut?' I asked. 'What does that mean?'

'We will just shut the doors and leave everything inside for you both,' the owner explained. 'You will need furniture and a lot of help, so we are more than happy to bless you in this way. Come, let's have a look around the house and see the furniture.'

I stood up in a state of shock and the owner's wife took me by the hand. 'Let's start in the kitchen,' she said, excitedly. 'So, we will leave the cooker and the fridge freezer and the table and chairs. Oh, and obviously all the built-in kitchen cupboards.'

'Oh, my goodness, thank you so much,' I exclaimed.

'No problem,' she replied. 'I was going to take the fridge freezer, but you will need it, that's for sure, especially if you are going to receive teams.'

The couple led us around the house, going into all the different rooms and showing us the beds and sofas and chairs.

'This is all yours,' the owner's wife declared. 'We are leaving it with our love.'

We also went onto the veranda, and they offered to leave us the beautiful wicker garden furniture as well.

The only furniture we needed to buy was wardrobes and a cot for Benjamin. The couple hugged us and prayed with us, and we left the house overwhelmed by God's faithfulness and provision.

The following week my dear mother-in-law gave us a cheque to buy the cot and the rest of the nursery furniture, and my parents sent a cheque for a pushchair for Benjamin.

A few weeks later we moved into our new home, a miracle home, provided by God and by very special people alert to His prods!

Questions

1. Do you have a testimony of God's financial provision in your life?

2. If God calls you to serve Him in long-term missions, how do you feel about trusting Him to provide for you/your family?

3. Do you have a testimony of when God provided for you in a way you didn't expect?

4. 'We don't give in order to receive; we give because we have received.' Reflect on that statement.

5. Is there someone in your family or close to you who is in need? How can you help them?

6. How can you be more expectant of God's goodness and provision?

Click on the QR code to watch the video about this chapter

Chapter Fourteen:

Be Specific

*And I will do whatever you ask in my name, so that
the Father may be glorified in the Son. You may ask
me for anything in my name, and I will do it.*

(John 14:13-14)

I have learned to be specific in the way I pray. I know exactly what I need and so does God! I have also learned to trust Him for all different areas of life such as health, family, finances, as well as ministry, of course.

For example, a friend came to me recently and said she was struggling at work with a difficult and unfair manager. She had reached her limit and had decided that if the manager didn't leave, then she would feel forced to resign. This was my prayer: 'Lord, please take care of this situation and if it is Your will, please move this person on. Give them a better job or some other reason for leaving and help my friend to be in peace. Thank You, Lord! Amen.'

I had great delight in receiving the news two days later that the manager who was causing the difficulty had decided to leave! Well, we prayed, didn't we?

I have seen God answer this kind of prayer many times for myself and for my friends and family, who always joke, 'Don't get on the wrong side of Cally!'

I am also constantly overwhelmed by God's creativity in answering my prayers. Money comes from the most unusual places and God often does the most incredible things to help me out.

When I left Milton Keynes for Brazil in 1999, I decided to rent out my house until it was the right time to sell it. I hit a barrier, however, when I discovered that the building society who gave me my mortgage were not in agreement, as I had no way of guaranteeing my mortgage payments if the people renting the house moved out.

Now I was stuck. I had to fill out a form and write a letter, and this paperwork was sent to the head office. I prayed and asked God to do a miracle. I had no idea how He was going to answer this prayer, but if it was His will for me to go to Brazil, I trusted Him to sort it out.

I heard nothing for a few weeks and then one afternoon received a phone call. It was from a manager at the head office asking to speak to me. She asked me if I was still intending to rent out my house and I confirmed that I was.

My heart was beating fast as I realised that the outcome of this conversation might mean the difference between me being able to go to Brazil or not. If I couldn't pay the mortgage from the rental payments, I would have to sell the house before I left, which could delay my departure by several months or more.

'Well, I have to tell you the building society does not usually permit you to rent out your house, and as manager of this department the decision is up to me,' she explained.

I held my breath, wondering what she was going to say. If the building society wasn't in agreement, what would make her want to help me?

'Please, Lord, do a miracle,' I prayed. I took a long, deep breath and waited.

Suddenly her tone of voice changed completely, and she said, 'Hi, Cally, this is Brigit!'

'Brigit?' I replied, feeling very confused.

'Yes, Brigit, from Estonia. Remember me?'

'Brigit? From Estonia?' I thought hard. Yes, I had met her there while I was doing the YWAM Discipleship Training School in 1994. She was a lovely young Estonian girl, full of love and zeal for the Lord. But what was she doing working at the head office of an English building society?

'Yes, of course I remember you,' I replied. 'Um . . . uh . . .' I could hardly get the words out. 'But how come you're phoning me, Brigit?' I was so confused. *Brigit, Estonia, my mortgage . . .* I thought to myself, 'What is going on?'

'I got married to Alex, remember?' she replied. 'And we're living in the UK. I have been working at the building society head office for several years and now I am manager of one of the departments. Your application form and letter happened to fall on my desk and when I saw your name, I decided to phone you. I am the person responsible for making the decision about your mortgage and I would like to let you know that the decision is yes.'

I nearly fainted in delight. This was truly amazing. God had certainly pulled out all the stops for this miracle to happen. I tried to process it all in my mind. Brigit, a young Estonian woman working in the UK, just 'happened' to be in exactly the right job at exactly the right time for me to get my mortgage approved so I could go to Brazil. How amazing is that?

'Brigit!' I exclaimed. 'Thank you. This is just so incredible. I'm in a state of shock,' I said, sitting down on the chair beside the phone, my legs like jelly.

'I am so happy to be able to help, Cally,' she replied enthusiastically. 'I hope you have a wonderful time in Brazil. I will be praying for you.'

'Thank you, Brigit, thank you so much,' I said, still hardly able to believe what had just happened. I hung up the phone and burst into tears with gratitude for this miracle that God had just worked. A few weeks later all the paperwork was complete, and I received the permission I needed to rent out my house.

What a faithful God we serve. I am telling you this story because I want you to know that if God is in something, He will move mountains to make it happen. As I look back over these last twenty-four years here in Brazil, I can see His hand upon my life so powerfully. A little thing like a building society hitch is nothing for Him, and I just love the way He used Brigit as an extra-special element in the story.

Running Associação Águia (The Eagle Project) here in Brazil is certainly a challenge and involves so much bureaucracy and red tape. In order to move forward and develop the project, we must jump through many hoops; it really is quite unbelievable. The problem is that so many of the organisations are corrupt and involved in money laundering, so the government makes it as difficult as possible to do anything.

One government registration, called the CMDCA,[23] is essential when making applications for funding from Brazilian companies and was proving especially difficult for us to acquire. With this document, the company can offset the donation from their taxes and so it encourages companies to give to charity organisations, which would be very helpful for us.

We applied for this registration during the COVID-19 pandemic, and it took nine months to receive a reply. We were refused the certificate because we were unable to provide the necessary fire service report for our headquarters. Unfortunately,

---

23. Conselho Municipal de Crianças e Adolescentes (The Municipal Council of Children and Adolescents).

this was impossible to obtain as all the departments were closed because of the pandemic. Then we discovered that it was more complicated than we thought as the building which houses our office space also didn't have the necessary fire service report, but only an engineer's statement. It seemed we were completely stuck and didn't know how to find a solution. This had been going on for months and was so frustrating, as we desperately wanted to move forward as an organisation.

I was due to go on a women's retreat with my church and was praying before I left my home. My church is very large with around 6,000 members and so I decided to ask God for a miracle.

'Lord, I need to get this registration,' I prayed. 'I do not know what to do any more. Please put someone in my path this weekend who can help me. In Jesus' name. Amen.'

I had no idea how God was going to answer this prayer but could never have imagined the way it would work out.

I arrived at the retreat and met many lovely women on the first evening. Being a member of such a huge church, it is difficult to get to know people and this was a wonderful opportunity. I remembered my prayer and was wondering if I was going to meet someone to help me with the registration.

The next day, I decided to go for a walk. It was a beautiful afternoon, and the sun was warm on my face and neck. I began to walk up a slight slope towards the farmyard area, and I began to chat to a woman walking in the same direction. We shared about our families and work, and she told me she was a biologist working in a laboratory in the centre of São Paulo. She had a lot of understanding about the COVID-19 vaccines and we had a very interesting chat. It was obvious she wouldn't be the one to help me with my urgent need, but I decided to ask her to pray.

'Could I ask you a favour?' I said.

'Yes, of course,' she replied.

'I desperately need to find a way to get a registration called the CMDCA and wonder if you would pray, please?'

'CMDCA?' she asked.

'From her tone of voice, it seems she knows what I'm talking about,' I thought. 'However, being a biologist, it's obvious she won't know how to help.'

'Yes,' I said out loud, sighing deeply. 'It's such a crazy situation. I can't believe this one registration is proving so difficult for us to obtain. It's essential for us to be able to get funding and we just can't get through the red tape.'

'Oh, isn't that funny,' she replied. 'I was talking to a friend of mine this week who runs a charity, and he is having the same kind of struggle with the CMDCA registration. I have his number, if you would like to contact him?'

'Oh, yes, please,' I exclaimed. 'That would be amazing. Maybe he can give me some ideas or suggestions. Thank you so much.'

'Well,' I thought. 'I wasn't expecting my new biologist friend to have the answer to my prayer but thank You, Lord.'

The following week I contacted her friend and explained the situation. I couldn't believe his reply.

'Cally, I have the phone number of the president of the CMDCA. Why don't you phone her and ask her how to proceed?'

'You have the phone number of the president of the CMDCA?' I exclaimed, shouting rather too loudly down the phone. 'That is amazing. Thank you so much. Maybe now we can get things moving!'

'I really hope so, Cally, so happy to help,' he said.

Now I had the president's phone number, but all I needed was the courage to phone her. I prayed for a few days and then summoned up the courage. The beginning of the phone call was a bit tense as she asked me different questions about our documents. I told her about our problem with the engineer's report and explained a little about the project. I told her how we use psychodrama in the youth prisons, and suddenly I could sense a change in her voice.

'Cally, your project sounds amazing,' she said. 'That is just the kind of project we are looking for at the CMDCA. But tell me, is this your first application?

'Yes,' I replied, wondering what she was going to say next.

'Then you don't need the fire service report, or the engineer's statement,' she said.

'I don't?'

'No, listen, send me all the other documents,' she said reassuringly. 'I will check everything is OK and then, when you send it to the CMDCA, copy me in on the message and I will make sure everything goes through smoothly.'

I was elated. After all this time struggling to obtain fire service reports and engineer's statements, finally, we would be able to obtain the registration.

'Thank you so much, I am so relieved,' I told her.

'No trouble at all, Cally, and please let me know if there is anything else I can do to help.'

I sent off all the documents and a few weeks later received the reply. Our application had been accepted, but they still insisted that we needed to provide the fire service report. I couldn't believe it. Surely we weren't back to square one again? Now, however, I had the president's number. I phoned her and she reassured me she would contact the department the following day to cancel this requirement.

Two days later we received our certificate! Phew. What a battle, but God once again made the miracle happen and put someone literally in my path to help.

Living by faith, as a missionary, is a privilege and an adventure. I am always so impressed by the way God provides through sometimes the most unusual of circumstances.

In 2020 *Dancing With Thieves* was published, and I needed the money to pay for the publishing contract. The final payment was for £1,000, and I didn't know how I was going to be able to pay. I was supporting my son at university in the UK and literally praying for every single pound that I needed to cover all my costs here in Brazil, as well as his university fees. Looking back, it was a time that really stretched my faith and I saw God doing miracles on almost a daily basis.

This last payment, however, was a challenge. I needed to pay my son's fees and the final publishing payment in the same week. I prayed and decided to pay the university fees. That meant that I didn't have the money for the publishing payment. I needed a miracle.

A few days later I received a message from someone I don't know, who was a friend of my neighbour, Pam, who lived next door to my family house in St Albans, England. Pam and her husband, Richard, were a lovely couple and became good friends to me and my parents; such good friends that one summer, when I was fifteen, they took me on holiday with them to the south of France. It was an amazing experience, my first time abroad, and we had a very special time together. Pam told me later that they considered me like the daughter they'd never had.

Richard had sadly died several years before, but I kept in touch with Pam and visited her on my last trip to the UK in the care home where she was a resident for the last years of her life. That visit turned out to be a small miracle, too. I was visiting a friend in Sussex and knew that Pam was in a home in the same county. However, I didn't know if it would be a long drive, so just as I left my friend's house, I looked up her address. I had decided that if it wasn't too far, I would go and visit. To my delight, the home was just 1 kilometre away! I dropped in as a surprise, and she was so delighted to see me. She was already very elderly and becoming frail, and I wondered how many more visits we would enjoy together.

Her friend contacted me a few months later to let me know she had passed away peacefully. I was so sad, but I believe she's with the Lord and was so glad that I made the effort to visit her that last time.

This same friend of Pam's contacted me again, the same week I needed the £1,000 to pay the publishing contract. She wanted to let me know some news. To my huge surprise, Pam had left me some money in her will! I was so shocked, as she had a son who was still alive, and I would never have imagined she would leave me something.

The friend explained that she was working through all the documents, but that in the next few days she would send me the money. You must be wondering how much it was? Yes, you guessed it – £1,000! That money blessed me so much, enabling me to pay the rest of the publishing contract and finally publish my first book.

I want to encourage you to be specific in your prayers. Our loving, wonderful, faithful heavenly Father longs to bless us. When we ask in faith and He answers, then we don't only get blessed, we have the opportunity to glorify Him with our testimony.

Questions

1. How do you feel about the whole subject of specific prayer?
2. Do you have a testimony of when you prayed very specifically, and God answered your prayer?

3. God might want to use us to be the answer to someone's specific prayer. How can we be more open to hear the Holy Spirit when He nudges us?

4. Is there a specific prayer you would like God to answer? Reflect and pray.

5. What should we do if God doesn't answer our prayer straightaway?

6. What does the Bible say about waiting on God? Which scriptures will help us in the waiting time?

Click on the QR code to watch the video about this chapter

Chapter Fifteen:

Be Ready to Stop

The first question which the priest and the Levite asked
was: 'If I stop to help this man, what will happen to me?'
But . . . the good Samaritan reversed the question: 'If I do
not stop to help this man, what will happen to him?'[24]

Life goes by so fast, doesn't it? One minute it's January, then it
seems we are celebrating Christmas again! My life here in São
Paulo is so busy, sometimes too busy, and I often feel rather
overwhelmed with just trying to keep everything running
smoothly.

Occasionally, though, something happens that brings me
back to my senses and shows me how important it is to slow
down, stop and help someone in need.

In 2014 I was returning home with George after a meeting in
São Paulo. The motorway was full of cars, which is normal for
a Sunday afternoon in São Paulo, as I have mentioned before in
this book. It is called 'the dormitory city' as so many residents
leave their homes on Friday evening and spend the weekend
away, only returning on Sunday afternoon. The traffic was
heavy but moving quite fast and we were about forty minutes
from home.

---

24. Martin Luther King Jr, in Clayborne Carson, *The Autobiography of Martin Luther King,
Jr.* (New York: Grand Central Publishing, 2001).

Suddenly I saw the red brake lights of the lorry in front of us and a motorcyclist being dragged across the ground into the right-hand lane of the motorway.

'Stop, George!' I shouted. 'Pull over to the hard shoulder, quick!'

George braked hard and screeched to a halt. Without thinking, I jumped out of the car and raced along the hard shoulder. The scene before me was one I will never forget. The lorry had run over the motorcyclist and the wheel of the lorry was still on top of his leg.

I can't even remember what I screamed to the lorry driver, but he carefully reversed, and the motorcyclist was now in a crumpled heap. He was lying on his side so I couldn't see the extent of his injuries, but he was obviously in terrible pain. He was slim, of about medium height and in his early thirties. He was dressed in full motorbike gear and was trying to remove his helmet.

I helped him and then knelt beside him and said, 'My name's Cally, and we're here to help you, OK? What's your name?'

'Marco,' he replied. His voice was firm, but I could tell he was very distressed. Other passers-by had also stopped, as well as the lorry driver, who was visibly shaken, and one of the onlookers, who was phoning the ambulance service.

'Help will soon be here,' I reassured him. 'Where are you hurt?'

'Just my leg,' he said, his voice shaking. 'I'm in so much pain!'

'You're going to be OK,' I reassured him. 'The ambulance is on its way. Can I phone a family member for you?'

He managed to pull his mobile phone out of the pocket of his leather motorcycle jacket and showed me his brother's phone number in the address list.

I phoned the number and a man answered with a friendly voice.

'Hello, hello? Who is it?'

'Oh, hi, my name is Cally,' I replied, 'and I'm here with your brother, on the Marginal Pinheiros. I'm very sorry to inform you that he has suffered a motorbike accident and we're waiting for the ambulance to arrive.'

There was a pause and then the line went dead.

'Hello? Hello? Are you there?' I asked. 'That's strange, Marco, I think he hung up on me!'

'Yeah, he probably thinks it's a scam,' Marco replied. 'Phone again and I'll talk to him.'

I phoned the number once more and Marco's brother answered the call again. I handed the phone to Marco, who explained what was happening. I later discovered that his brother thought that maybe I was someone trying to extort money out of him. That is quite common in Brazil. People phone you to inform you that they are with one of your relatives after a car accident and then when you go rushing to the scene, you are robbed.

'He said he's on his way,' Marco explained. His voice was fainter now and strained, and I was very concerned for him.

'Marco, I am a Christian. Could I pray for you?' I asked.

'Oh, yes, please.'

I prayed for God to ease the pain and bring him comfort. He sighed deeply and seemed to be more peaceful. He told me later that the pain subsided after I prayed, and he stopped fearing that he was going to die.

The minutes passed by, and the ambulance still didn't arrive. It felt like an eternity. I was so desperate for Marco to get help and be taken to hospital. His brother arrived and was obviously very upset. He explained that Marco was travelling home after a weekend away with about twenty motorbike riders. He was the leader of the group and responsible for seeing everyone safely on their way at the end of the trip. He had just waved the last rider goodbye when a car touched the side of his bike and knocked him in front of the lorry.

I prayed and prayed for the ambulance to come. The minutes went ticking by and still it didn't arrive. It was now late afternoon, but the sun was still hot on my neck. My knees ached from kneeling for so long on the gravel, but I wasn't going to leave Marco until help arrived.

After about fifty long minutes, I heard a siren and suddenly the ambulance screeched to a halt on the right lane of the motorway beside us. Marco breathed a huge sigh of relief as the two paramedics appeared at his side.

After a quick explanation of what had happened, they began to turn Marco onto his back. I stood up, grateful for the opportunity to stretch my legs, hardly able to walk as the backs of my knees were so taut and stiff.

As the paramedics gently turned Marco onto his back his injured leg was exposed, and I saw the extent of his injuries. By this time, I was now standing up beside George and I turned my eyes away towards his shoulder.

'No!' I whispered. 'His leg will have to be amputated!'

'Not necessarily,' George whispered back. 'They can do amazing things with this kind of injury.'

'He certainly is going to need a miracle,' I thought to myself.

The skin on the front of Marco's thigh was completely open and his leg was like a mass of raw minced beef. I winced as the paramedics began to wrap his leg in bandages.

'We're going to have to get this jacket off,' the paramedic announced, taking out a large pair of scissors and kneeling beside Marco's chest.

'Oh, please don't cut my jacket,' Marco said, his voice shaking with emotion. 'Do you really have to? It's just my leg that's injured.' It was obviously very important to him, and I was amused that he seemed more concerned about losing his jacket than about his leg.

'I don't think he has upper body injuries,' I explained. 'Couldn't you leave it just until he gets to the hospital?'

'Nah, sorry, it needs to come off,' the paramedic replied sternly.

'Please!' Marco was now really upset. 'Please don't cut it off.'

The paramedic paused. I wondered how many times a day he was faced with this situation. The statistics of motorbike accidents in São Paulo are horrifying, with hundreds of fatal accidents every year.

'OK, keep calm,' he replied. 'We'll see what we can do.'

They lifted Marco onto the stretcher and carried him into the ambulance. Cars and motorbikes were driving past us, motorists staring out of their car windows, obviously curious to know what was happening. I wondered if Marco would ever ride a motorbike again.

I turned to his brother and asked for his phone number so we could keep in contact and find out about Marco's progress. His brother hugged us, obviously extremely worried.

'Thank you so much for looking after Marco and staying with him all this time. I really appreciate it,' he said.

'Please, you don't need to thank us,' I said. 'We're just so glad we were here to help.'

We walked back down the motorway in the direction of our car. My heart was heavy, and I began to cry, overwhelmed with the emotion of the afternoon. We got into the car and George turned the key in the ignition.

Nothing.

He tried again.

Nothing.

He had left the emergency lights flashing the whole time we were with Marco and now the car battery was dead!

Marco's brother was parked behind us, and George ran to ask for his help. He fortunately had jump leads in his car and quickly helped us. Praise God! It would have been complicated if he hadn't been there to rescue us.

The next day I phoned Marco's mobile phone, and his mum answered the call. I held my breath, not knowing what she would say.

Would Marco have lost his leg? Would the surgeon have been able to save it? Would he ever walk again? So many questions ran through my mind.

'Hi, this is Cally, I'm the person who was with Marco after the accident yesterday. I'm just wondering how he's doing?'

'Oh, I want to thank you so much,' she replied. 'Thank you for helping my son. He said you were like a guardian angel, and he doesn't know if he would have survived without you.'

'I am so glad I was able to help. How is he?'

'He's here beside me. He had an operation on his injured leg last night. The surgeon took a skin graft from his hip and was able to save his leg.' Her voice shook with emotion. 'He will need more operations, but things are going well so far.'

'Oh, that is such good news!' I exclaimed. 'I was so worried he would lose his leg. It didn't look too good yesterday on the side of the motorway.'

'Yes, we are all so relieved. Please come and visit him in the hospital when you can.' She gave me the details of the hospital address and room number and I promised to visit as soon as possible.

A week or so later I was in the area so dropped by to see him. I popped my head round the door of his room and saw him propped up in bed with his mother sitting on a chair beside him.

'Hiya,' I said. 'Surprise! How are you doing?'

Marco's face broke into a huge smile, and he announced, 'My guardian angel! Oh, it's so good to see you!'

'And it is very good to see you,' I replied, 'and looking so well.' I gave Marco a huge hug and then hugged his mum and sat down on a chair at the end of the bed. I didn't stay long, but it was long enough to meet Marco properly instead of lying injured on the motorway.

That was the beginning of a strong friendship with him and his family members. He is like a brother to me, and I have been invited to be part of their family celebrations on different occasions. I was one of the matrons of honour at Marco's wedding to Daniela, was invited to the baptism of their son, and my sons and I have been part of several Christmas and birthday celebrations. It is such a special relationship to have come out of what could have been a tragic accident.

Marco recovered miraculously well. He walks without a limp and leads a completely normal life. Just a few centimetres' difference and the lorry would have run over his abdomen, chest or head and the story would have had a very different ending.

One other very special outcome from this relationship is that Marco and Dani generously donate towards food parcels for The Eagle Project every month. Marco says, 'It is just a small way of showing my eternal gratitude to you.'

I could never have imagined that stopping on the motorway that day would have brought so many blessings. I certainly didn't expect anything in return, but God has blessed me so much through this relationship.

Don't let life become so busy that you don't have the time or energy to stop. Every time we put God first and help someone that He puts in our path, we can be assured that we are extending the kingdom of God and being used as an instrument in His hands. That isn't a burden, that is a privilege. That is one way we can break the vase of our life and allow the love to spill out, a 'love that can't be contained'.

Questions

1. Do you have a testimony of when you stopped to help someone? What happened?

2. Have you ever been in a situation where someone needed help and you didn't stop? What could you have done differently?

3. Have you ever had the experience of someone stopping to help you? How did that feel?

4. Have you had the experience of needing help and no one stopping to help you?

5. Spend some time reading the parable of the Good Samaritan in Luke 10:25-37.

6. Reflect on that Bible story. How might you feel if someone offered to help you that you really didn't expect to offer assistance?

Click on the QR code to watch the video about this chapter

Final Words

I have a deep sense of excitement about this book. I am picturing you reading this book alone, or as part of a small-group study, and am imagining the thoughts you have had after reading each chapter, answering the questions and watching the videos.

Maybe you have never given your life to Christ, and I would like to give you an invitation. When I first started working with the street kids in São Paulo, I used to visit several families on a regular basis who lived in the north of the city. After several months of visits and Bible studies, one of the women asked me, 'Cally, when are you going to ask me if I want to give my life to Jesus?'

Taken aback, I replied, 'You want to give your life to Jesus?'

'Yes!' she said. 'I was just waiting for you to ask.'

So, before I finish writing this book, I would like to ask you:

Would you like to make a commitment to follow Jesus?

Maybe you have never made a commitment to follow Him, and might be wondering, 'Where do I begin?'

Here are some simple steps to help you:

Step 1 – Admit your need for Jesus as your Lord and Saviour.
We all need to admit that we are separated from God because of our sins, the things we have done wrong (Romans 3:23). The

good news is that Jesus' death on the cross paid for all our sins and through Him we have access to God, and to eternal life with Him (John 3:16).

Step 2 – **Ask** for forgiveness.

We need to ask God to forgive us and help us to forgive those who have hurt us. He promises that when we do this we are 'born again' as a new creation: 'Therefore, if anyone is in Christ, the new creation has come: the old has gone, the new is here!' (2 Corinthians 5:17). So, we have a brand-new start! The Bible says, 'I have been crucified with Christ and I no longer live, but Christ lives in me. The life I now live in the body, I live by faith in the Son of God, who loved me and gave himself for me' (Galatians 2:20). That's good news!

Step 3 – **Accept** God's forgiveness and that you need His help.

We need to know that we are forgiven, and that God will help us to change and to walk with Him the rest of our lives.

Step 4 – **Pray this prayer:**

Dear Lord Jesus,

I want to give my life to You. Thank You that You created me and that I am Your child.

Please forgive me for all the things I have done wrong, and please help me to follow You all of my days.

I receive Your forgiveness and ask You to help me forgive those who have hurt me or harmed me in some way.

Please fill me with Your Holy Spirit and lead me and guide me for the rest of my life.

Amen.

Well done! Remember today's date – it's your new birthday!
(See 2 Corinthians 5:17.)

Step 4 – Act!

Becoming a Christian isn't just praying a prayer. Now you need to grow in your faith and step into the plans God has for your life. I want to encourage you to look for a church as close to where you live as possible, somewhere where you will feel at home. There are so many different styles of churches and there will certainly be one that suits your personality and needs.

Find out about house groups – groups that meet during the week for Bible study, prayer and fellowship – and join one. Read the Bible and pray.

This is just the beginning of a new and exciting journey for you with God. He has wonderful plans to work in you and through you!

God bless you!

'For I know the plans I have for you,' declares the LORD, 'plans to prosper you and not to harm you, plans to give you hope and a future. Then you will call on me and come and pray to me, and I will listen to you. You will seek me and find me when you seek me with all your heart.'

(Jeremiah 29:11-13)

Finally, to you all, I pray you are inspired and encouraged to step out for Jesus and break the alabaster vase of your life for Him. I also pray you have new ideas and strategies to reach those He places in your path and are already seeing the fruit of this new journey. My heart leaps with joy to think of all the people who will be blessed through your lives.

I want to end with one more encouragement to *be*.

This one is very important.

I want to encourage you to *be you*! God has equipped you and given you certain gifts and qualities that make you unique and who you are, in Him and for Him. He has a special plan and journey for you, and my prayer is that you will step out in faith and trust Him, every step of the way.

Always remember that you never need to do anything in your own strength as His Holy Spirit is with you, anointing you and empowering you. Allow His love to spill out of the vase of your life and believe that He will keep filling you to overflowing, to keep loving and serving Him with all that you are.

In the introduction to this book, I wrote:

Are you willing to pour out the perfume of your life, breaking your vase of love without restraint, radically, wholeheartedly and unashamedly? Are you ready to give yourself to Jesus, allowing His fragrance in your life to powerfully permeate the lives of others? Are you willing to live for Him? Are you also prepared to risk stepping out for Him and trust that He will take care of you?

I pray that this book has indeed encouraged you to step out and love others more with a deeper understanding of God's love for you.

Be ready
Be willing
Be expectant
Be open.
Be all that He has made you to *be*... so a 'love that can't be contained' will well up inside you and flow out of you and through you to the broken world around you.

May God be gracious to us and bless us
and make his face shine on us –
so that your ways may be known on earth,
your salvation among all nations.
May the peoples praise you, God;
may all the peoples praise you.
May the nations be glad and sing for joy,
for you rule the peoples with equity
and guide the nations of the earth.
May the peoples praise you, God;
may all the peoples praise you.
The land yields its harvest;
God, our God, blesses us.
May God bless us still,
so that all the ends of the earth will fear him.

(Psalm 67)

Click on the QR code to watch the video about this chapter

Acknowledgements

To my sons, Benjamin and Joseph – thank you for all your love. The way you encourage me and support me means everything. I love you both with all my heart.

To my UK publishers, Malcolm and Sarah at Malcolm Down and Sarah Grace Publishing, and my Brazilian publishers, Josiane and Claudio at Editora Esperança. Thank you for believing in me and for all your encouragement to keep writing, to keep stretching my wings and allowing me to fly.

To Sheila Jacobs for editing this book, for all your input and attention to detail, you are amazing!

To Jennifer, for all the coaching sessions, especially on helping me organise my time to get this book to completion.

To Steve Murrill, for being such an incredible example and mentor to me.

To Eloir, my dear friend. Thank you for all your love and friendship, and thank you in advance for translating this book into Portuguese.

Thank you to all my friends and family members (you know who you are), who constantly encourage me and make me feel so loved.

To all the School of Supernatural Life team and speakers who inspire me and spur me on.[25]

Thank you to my dear friends from Itapetininga – Raquel Izumi, and Bob and Greice Almeida for all the help and technical support: Gabriel Pranches for the song recording, Rafael Oliveira Fructuoso de Siqueira, and Marcos Adriano de Abreu for the guitar accompaniment and arrangement. Also a huge thank you to Fábio Machado for editing the videos.

25. The School of Supernatural Life (SSL) is hosted by the New Life Church in Milton Keynes and they have offered this course for many years. During the COVID-19 pandemic they invited me to participate, as it is now online and therefore, I could take part from Brazil. I am now a group coach and guest speaker. It is truly transformational. For more information, see www.sslmk.org (accessed 16 January 2023).

Appendix One

A woman knelt, at Jesus' feet
A broken vessel she held in her hand
And she poured out her life
A fragrant perfume her sacrifice.

And the people laughed and jeered.
They laughed in her face.
They said that money could
have been used for the poor.
And they laughed at her
They said 'What a waste!'
But she knew what it was for.

As she poured out her life
She gave everything for her Lord.
Her whole life outpoured.
As she poured out her life
She gave everything for her Lord
Her whole life outpoured.

And so, I sit, at Jesus feet.
A broken vessel in His hands
And I pour out my life
All I am for Him, my sacrifice.

And if people laugh and jeer
If they laugh in my face.
If they say my life could
have been used for something more
If they laugh at me
If they say 'What a waste!'
I'll tell them who I'm living for.

As I pour out my life
I give everything for my Lord.
My whole life outpoured.
As I pour out my life
I give everything for my Lord
My whole life outpoured.
As I pour out my life
I give them everything for my Lord
My whole life outpoured.

Cally Magalhães
September 1994

Further Information

For further information about The Eagle Project/Associação Águia:

www.theeagleproject.co.uk
www.associacaoaguia.org.br

or contact Cally at:
callyjcm@gmail.com

Instagram: @cally_magalhaes
              @aguiaassociacao

Facebook: https://www.facebook.com/The-Eagle-Project-
             170502183081714/
Portuguese: https://www.facebook.com/associacaoaguia/

The Eagle Project and Cally depend on one-off and regular donations.
If you would like information about how to support The Eagle Project and/or Cally, please contact Stewardship at:

enquiries@stewardship.org.uk

Or
https://my.give.net/eagle

The Eagle Project: Ref. 20098650
Cally's personal/family support: Ref. 20035365

Made in the USA
Monee, IL
17 October 2023

44671040R00103